Dear Mike,

Thank you for enriching
my mother's final days.

Love you cous,
Christine Taylor

And Then There Was
Light

My Journey through Mental Illness

And Then There Was

Light

CHRISTINE TAYLOR

LifeRich
PUBLISHING

LifeRich Publishing is a registered trademark of The Reader's Digest Association, Inc.

LifeRich Publishing books may be ordered through booksellers or by contacting:

LifeRich Publishing
1663 Liberty Drive
Bloomington, IN 47403
www.liferichpublishing.com
1 (888) 238-8637

Because of the dynamic nature of the Internet, any web addresses or links contained in this book may have changed since publication and may no longer be valid. The views expressed in this work are solely those of the author and do not necessarily reflect the views of the publisher, and the publisher hereby disclaims any responsibility for them.

Any people depicted in stock imagery provided by Thinkstock are models, and such images are being used for illustrative purposes only.
Certain stock imagery © Thinkstock.

ISBN: 978-1-4897-1068-0 (sc)
ISBN: 978-1-4897-1069-7 (hc)
ISBN: 978-1-4897-1067-3 (e)

Library of Congress Control Number: 2017901865

Print information available on the last page.

LifeRich Publishing rev. date: 2/20/2017

Dedication

*T*his book is dedicated to all people who deal with mental illness on a personal or professional level or through their association with family and/or friends. And finally, I dedicate this book to my husband, Arthur, and my mother, Marie, who were supportive throughout my many years of depression. Unfortunately, my husband and my mother died prior to the time I came into the light.

Acknowledgements

I would first like to acknowledge my editor, my tenth-grade English teacher, Mr. Bruce Laddie, and his lovely wife, Ruth for reviewing and editing this manuscript. They have helped with rounding out the thought processes and refining the meaning of my book. I could not have done without their patience, diligence, persistence, encouragement, love, and refined knowledge. This book would not be the book it is without their input. I was blessed to have Mr. Laddie as a teacher and as a lifelong friend. His fine wife allowed him the hundreds of hours that he took to review and revise this manuscript, for which I am very grateful. Bruce turned ninety years old this past October while working on this memoir. Happy 90th birthday, Bruce!

After Bruce edited the book, I handed the manuscript which I had re-entered into the computer to one of my choir members for a final proofreading. Eileen Mays is not only a beautiful person and a great alto singer but also a great editor. She helped to refine the memoir even further by editing out some of the redundancy and adding many commas. I am truly thankful for her help with this book.

Again I re-edited the book with Eileen's recommendations. My neighbor Inna Peters wanted to read the book. She located the typos in the manuscript for the third and final edit. She was both encouraging and helpful.

Individuals who encouraged me to write this book include Dr. Dave, my psycho-pharmacologist and psychotherapist; Rae, my sister; and Mitch Bridges who works in a think tank in Boston, MA. Their encouragement lead to the three-year process of writing this book, something I would never have thought of doing.

I thank God for His inspiration, which I needed for the self-confidence I never had until recent years, and for making all things come together in my life.

Contents

Preface

I have been told to write this book on three separate occasions. Three is a magic number in my life; things tend to happen in threes: three births, three deaths, three moves, three grandchildren. And then, of course, there is the Trinity.

The one significant thing that did not happen in threes was the seesawing of my moods; this happened mostly in two-week intervals. The problem was not so much that my mood cycled; it was that events would happen in two-week periods, thus affecting my mood. I would have two weeks of routine life events and then all hell would break loose for the next two weeks, or a significant negative event would occur and it would take me two weeks to deal with it before my mood returned to stability, such as it was. These hellish mood swings were usually caused by behavior or health issues in my family or by work-related issues. My life was variable, a mix of many traumatic events countered by many blessings by God.

There were two significant turning points in my life between ages sixty-one and sixty-two: the revision of my mental health diagnosis and the implementation of nontraditional healing methods. Both events occurred due to the insightfulness of my amazing psychiatrist. If they had not happened, this book would not exist.

So why is my story unique? Many people overcome mental illness, or live a reasonable life despite it, through traditional treatment. What is significant is the way I overcame my mental illness.

Being in the light has helped me deal with many of life's challenges. Yes, I still have family issues and health problems, but the light has given me the ability to implement much of what I have learned over the years rather than resorting to self-loathing, incredible sadness, feelings of victimization and isolation, and significant mental anguish and anxiety.

I have written this book under my pen name, Christine Taylor, and have changed the names of my children and other characters. I removed some names altogether for clarity, used or changed the initials of some others to protect the identity of those I might offend, and changed the names and locations of some events for the sake of anonymity.

This story is true, and I've told it with as much accuracy as my memory allows. I have kept many journals over the years in order to capture the events, observations, and feelings I experienced. I have also consulted my college transcript, medical books and articles, and reliable individuals regarding dates of death and to confirm my interpretation of situations I describe in this memoir. In addition, I have found Internet research to be very helpful. I have asked the professionals, family, and friends cited here to review chapters of the book for truth and accuracy. Because I'm describing real-life events, some individuals may take umbrage with what I've written, but in no way did I intend to offend or criticize anyone.

Chapter 1

The Early Years
Part 1

*I*t was a cold winter day—Christmas Eve, 1950—when my mother gave birth to me at a major teaching hospital in Philadelphia. Although my delivery was long and arduous (I met the world feetfirst), it turned out to be a joyous occasion for my mother, Marie, who was thirty-four, and my father, Edwin, thirty-six. I was the first child for Marie and Ed, and they were delighted when I joined them. Mom always said, "I gave my husband something no one else could give him for Christmas."

On Christmas Day, my father proudly walked down the hallway of the large, sterile hospital carrying a small, decorated Christmas tree in one hand and a stocking in the other. After extracting bottles of lotion and perfume from the latter, my mother was surprised to find, nestled in the toe, a beautifully wrapped surprise: a platinum, channel-set diamond wedding band. That Christmas was unlike any other my parents would have for the rest of their lives. After all, what were the chances of another child being born on the same date, and how many diamond wedding bands does a woman receive from her only husband?

I seemed to be a very happy and healthy child at birth. I was the center of my parents' lives as well as the lives of my paternal grandparents, Edwin and Beth, who had waited thirty-six years before being blessed with a granddaughter from their only child. Everyone was happy that I had arrived, for it had taken some gynecological manipulations before my mother could get pregnant.

It was a joyous holiday season for my parents and grandparents—and the timing could not have been better from my perspective too. As I got older and understood that I had a Christmas birthday, I saw it as a special event. Although I never had a birthday party because of the complications of scheduling one around the holiday, I always felt special having a birthday near the day when we celebrate Christ's birth. Nevertheless, throughout my life, I have been asked, "Didn't you get cheated having your birthday at Christmas?" The answer is no, because my mother always made sure I had a beautiful Christmas/birthday cake and I always received something special from my parents.

Being the first grandchild of my paternal grandparents gave me a special position in the limelight. My grandfather, whom I called Pop-Pop, was a commercial photographer; therefore, it was logical that he took hundreds of black-and-white pictures of me, which he developed in a tiny darkroom in the basement of his narrow row house on Teesdale Street in Philadelphia. I can still remember the bright explosion of flashbulbs and the loud pop that followed the taking of each indoor picture. These photos, many of them duplicates and triplicates, now reside in cardboard boxes and plastic tubs in my son's basement, waiting for me to put them into family albums for my children. (When my sister, Rae, came along two years and eight months later, the novelty of taking baby pictures had worn off to a certain degree.)

Best of all, as time passed, I became my father's special little girl—a point that needs to be remembered. My father was a handsome man, standing five-feet-eleven and weighing about 145 pounds. He was a high school graduate, and when I was a youngster he took business classes in the evenings. He worked in one of the premier leather tanning companies in Philadelphia—it eventually closed around 1965—and his job as a foreman tanner ultimately led to his premature death. Despite being the head of his department, he earned a rather meager salary. But Daddy was a diligent worker and well regarded. He would get up at six o'clock in the morning and be at work by seven, usually returning home around dinnertime, before which he would shower, shave, put on clean clothes, and polish his shoes. On the side he sold jewelry, and he also became a Freemason. He was very handy and could fix almost anything (a quality not indigenous to all men, as I learned after I got married). He took care of cutting the grass and all plumbing, painting, wallpapering, and electrical projects around the house. Most of what he spent on home maintenance was for tools and building supplies rather than repairmen's bills, so our family saved a lot of money. Daddy also repaired automobiles; I remember him going to the junkyard and getting used parts when something needed to be replaced on one of our cars. One time he built a trellis for my mother to grow her large Concord grapes. He was a very hard worker.

My father adored me, and I grew to love him more than anyone else in the world. I would anxiously wait for him to come home from work just so I could give him a kiss and a big hug. As a toddler, I would join my parents in the living room each evening to watch our one and only TV, sitting on the burgundy-carpeted floor at their feet with my legs drawn up in the shape of a W—a position I can no longer attain at the age of sixty-five, even while doing yoga. According to family lore, at the age of two, I would sip my father's nightly beer (although I can no longer tolerate the taste of it). Sometimes both my parents read me bedtime stories, which I loved. *Heidi* was my favorite book when I was a little girl—I had practically memorized it, so there was no possibility that my parents could chance skipping a few pages now and then. I also remember kneeling at my bedside to say my goodnight prayers at the age of four or five.

My paternal grandmother, whom I always called Nana, came from a large family whose members were scattered throughout Pennsylvania, New Jersey, and Delaware. My sister and I visited them often over the years, usually in the company of Nana and Pop-Pop. Nana's family members were extraordinary people who freely shared their love, kindness, and generosity, and all of them could prepare wonderful meals. Many of them were well educated; all of them had finished high school, and some had graduated from college as well. Nana's one brother was the principal of a high school in Philadelphia, and his wife was a teacher. One of Nana's brothers-in-law was a Methodist minister, married to the perfect pastor's wife. Reverend Kay eventually became my mother's mentor; when life became difficult for her, he was her inspiration to keep going and love herself. I cared as deeply for my father's family as I did my mother's, though it seemed to me that my parents came from two different worlds.

My wonderful grandparents would often gather at our home for holiday meals. In one of Pop-Pop's photos, taken when I was about one, all four of my grandparents are sitting around the dining room table in our small ranch house in Pennsylvania, sharing a holiday meal my mother prepared. The picture speaks for itself: everyone at the table looks happy and comfortable. When the holidays came around, Mom always had my grandparents over for a turkey dinner, rising early in the morning to bake a pound cake and prepare stuffing with all the trimmings. Those holiday meals were always delicious. (It is rumored that I ate nineteen black olives at my first birthday dinner without choking or swallowing any of the pits. It's unlikely that I had room for anything else after that.) We used to laugh at Mom because after preparing the meal and cleaning up the kitchen, she invariably fell asleep on the couch, exhausted from all the work. Looking back at those occasions, I wonder if she ever had time to enjoy what she cooked, for she was always concentrating on making sure everyone *else* was happy and well fed.

My paternal grandparents had only one child—my father, Edwin. They had a long lineage in America; they were not first- or second-generation immigrants, like my mother's family. My Nana was Pennsylvania Dutch, and my Pop-Pop was probably of English and Irish heritage. Regardless, they considered themselves strictly Americans and rarely discussed their ancestry, which was of little significance to them.

Nana was a very slim and attractive lady who, after completing her housework each day, would bathe and then put on a perfectly ironed dress with jewelry (which she loved to wear) and makeup. She was a housewife who also cleaned her brother's home on Fridays, since he and his wife both worked and had no children to help with the household chores. Part of the reason she undertook this extra job was that my grandfather was inclined to be parsimonious, and cleaning her brother's home afforded her some extra pin money, which she usually spent on my sister and me.

My grandmother came from a large family, all of whom were very close and loving. My great-aunt Lori, a widow, often came to visit her sister, Beth; she would play games with me for hours. God bless her, she was quite the good sport!

My Nana taught me how to do handiwork, and one thing I will always remember about her is that whenever my sister and I visited her, she would give us a bag of goodies—bananas, candy, pretzels, and other treats. She also made the best pork and beans, pigs in a blanket, macaroni salad, and 7Up cake.

I didn't know it at the time, but Nana would become one of my guardian angels, for she was always there when I needed her. She loved me unconditionally, never uttered a word of criticism, and took care of me when no one else was around. Even now, I think of her every day. I dream of being a grandmother like my Nana.

I remember my paternal grandfather as an old man who was essentially bald, with a swath of white hair around the lower sides and back of his head and a few strands atop the crown. He had only one sibling, Margaret, and she was destined to die an old maid. Pop-Pop loved ice cream and sweets (a taste that perhaps I inherited from him). I remember him retiring at the age of seventy-two.

Early in my parents' marriage, in about 1939, they bought a house in Philadelphia proper, not far from Nana's and Pop-Pop's. Mom was proud of this corner house with its white tieback curtains and white picket fence, and she and Dad took meticulous care of the property. World War II necessitated my father's enlistment in the US Army. He was commissioned and sent to Georgia as a member of a quartermaster supply unit. While there, he divorced my mother and married a woman named Marsha. During that period, Mom found work as a hairdresser in an upscale department store in downtown Philadelphia. She also began collecting crystal and china—nice things that were important to her, as she'd been deprived of them growing up. She also enjoyed buying clothing for her mother. Mom managed to financially maintain this house during the war.

Even after my father remarried, my mother remained single. Then, at the war's end, my father divorced Marsha, and he remarried my mother in 1949. The fact that she would take him back was inexplicable to me, but it hinted at the possibility that she had never stopped loving him. Unfortunately, she failed to see the signs of bad things to come.

Upon my father's return and my parents' remarriage, my father returned to the house they had originally purchased near my grandparents'. It was while they were living there that Mom got pregnant with me in March 1950.

Shortly after I was born, Mom and Dad bought a Toll Brothers house in the Philadelphia suburbs. No doubt they saw this as a step up the ladder of success, for now they owned a house surrounded by a half acre of land. As was their habit, they took wonderful care of the house and worked hard on the adjoining lawn. They were, in other words, house-proud—a quality they instilled in me for life.

My sister, Rae, was born in August 1953, when my mother and

father were thirty-six and thirty-eight. In that era, children had much more freedom than what is considered permissible now. Rae and I were allowed to roam our environs to an extent that today would appear to border on parental neglect.

I had many playmates by the time I started kindergarten at the local elementary school, and I have fond memories of walking to school with my friends, playing on the schoolyard monkey bars, and swinging around the chinning bars. I loved school and learning. I must have had a great affinity for dinosaurs, for I was always looking at pictures of them in the encyclopedia. I also loved it when my mother would cut roses from her garden and give them to me to take to school, for I was always proud and happy to share them with my teacher.

We often attended a local Episcopal church as a family. I received a pin and then a wreath for excellent attendance, as I took both school and church very seriously. Dependability and excellence were instilled in me as a youngster; as a result, I have no memory of getting into trouble at home, school, or church—though I'm sure I was no angel!

Another thing we habitually did as a family was go to Acme grocery store for provisions every Saturday. Often we would purchase needed odds and ends from other stores at the same time. Sometimes on Saturday evenings we would go to the local firehouse, which had a bar. There Dad would have beer and Mom would have an old-fashioned, while my sister and I had cheese dogs and root beer. These customs always gave me a healthy sense of family normalcy.

At home, the main source of entertainment was our black-and-white console television set. I can remember watching *The Mickey Mouse Club* and *The Sally Starr Show,* which played Popeye cartoons and Three Stooges movies, while Mom prepared dinner. In those days there were only three channels, but we were never bored.

One of my grandfather's snapshots shows Rae and me in Halloween costumes—she was a clown and I was Uncle Sam—ready to go trick-or-treating with my father while Mom stayed home to hand out candy to other neighborhood kids. Mom laughingly reminded us years later that Rae always had the reputation of being stingy with her treats, refusing to share them with anyone. Another memory of Rae was of the time the township was installing underground sewers and she fell into one of the holes that had been dug for the pipes. With the help of some kind neighbors, she was rescued from the trenches. Her mishap was no surprise; she was always getting into some sort of mischief, which led my parents to refer to her as "a real pistol." Another fond memory of mine was of our across-the-street neighbors' good-sized swimming pool, which we were invited to use during the hot summer months.

My parents always decorated the house for Christmas. Dad would put up a train platform with trees, houses, a firehouse, a train station complete with people and benches, a school, a hospital, and a church. Mom later told me that although they purchased lots of Christmas toys for Rae and me, my father would cry because he wanted to have more presents for us under the tree.

Everything seemed perfect in my little world. I wanted for nothing. I was always well dressed, I lived in a nice house, and I never went hungry. I was also blessed with a loving father and mother and had an extended family of caring grandparents and aunts and uncles. In other words, we were an average post-World War II lower-middle-class family with a lot of pride and ambition.

The Early Years
Part 2

As I said, my parents came from two different worlds. My mother was born in 1916 in the city of Philadelphia to two Italian immigrants who had arrived at the Port of Philadelphia during the late 1800s. She was the third child in a very large family; there were a total of fifteen births, including some twins and triplets, but only eight of the children survived to adulthood. Mom would speak of the wakes her family held for those dead babies, recalling their tiny caskets resting on the dining room table. It must have been difficult for my mother's parents to have lost so many children.

Grandmom and Grandpop were both orphaned at a young age in the mountains of Italy. The exact place of origin was never revealed to me. What was shared with me was that my grandfather came to America at age sixteen and worked in a felt mill in Philadelphia, saving his money so that he could bring his girlfriend—my grandmother— and their respective families over from Italy. My grandparents (who had similar names, Joseph and Josephine) worked very hard to earn a living for their large family. Although they had a house, they had few possessions, and their main concern was feeding and clothing their children. They were proud and acculturated people who were never on the dole, even during the Great Depression.

My mom, Marie, was the first of my grandparents' children to be born in a hospital. Mom grew up in the Frankford section of Philadelphia. She was a beautiful little girl with dark-brown eyes and black, curly hair, and she grew up to be five feet and a quarter inch tall. (She always counted that quarter inch, which became significant when she began to shrink in her later years.) She spoke an Italian dialect that her parents taught her.

When she was young, Mom went to the local public elementary school, where she was the teacher's pet. Unfortunately, when the Great Depression hit, she was forced to quit school in the eighth grade and go to work. My mother both regretted and resented not being able to finish high school; she always felt inferior, especially around my father, because of her lack of formal education. As a result she would say to us children, "Get your education because no one can take that away from you"—a simple truth she repeated time and time again.

As a teenager she dutifully handed over her paycheck to her mother to help provide the bounty of food needed for their family of ten. Mom often spoke of the crates of eggs and sacks of flour that would be delivered to their house. My grandmother also grew many vegetables in her garden, and Mom would pick them to make dinner.

Grandmom made her own pasta and used fresh herbs and spices to season her food. Mom used to tell me that my grandmother cooked better than many of the gourmet cooks of today. Legend has it that one Christmas morning, my grandfather went to Mass wearing his spats and a top hat and carrying a cane. He arrived home to find that my grandmother had fallen asleep frying her delicious Christmas cookies. Thankfully, he'd come back just in time to prevent a monumental fire which could have burned down the house, including all the children who were on the upper floors, patiently waiting for my grandmother to bang her wooden spoon on the heating duct so they could come down and eat her delicious treats. Thank God for the arrival of my grandfather.

In addition to her flower, vegetable, and herb gardens, my grandmother also had three poodles that wore bows in their hair and ran up and down the alley by the house. Unfortunately, my grandmother's love for animals never carried over to my mother—although later in my mother's life, my sister, who was and still is an animal lover, brought home every injured animal, turtle, bird, and fish she could find. We even had a dog for a few weeks, until Dolly jumped up on a kitchen chair and ate the leftovers out of a pot that was sitting on the table. That was enough for my mother to take her to the SPCA the following day. Of course Rae and I were heartbroken.

I was just one of the many grandchildren my maternal grandparents had, but I always felt loved by them. My grandmother died of a ruptured gallbladder just before my second birthday, but my grandfather survived for several more years, living with my mother's oldest sibling, Adolph, and his second wife, Mary. I remember seeing Grand Pop when I'd visit my mother's siblings, most of whom lived in the Frankford section of Philadelphia. Since many of them didn't own a car or even know how to drive, my mother and father were usually the ones doing the traveling to visit them. Mom had one sister, Helen, who had been in the military during World War II and had moved to Florida with her military husband and two children. Our family rarely saw Aunt Helen, but Mom would visit her on occasion

My father and mother never shared with my sister and me the details of their meeting and marriage. However, documents I found in a metal box of my mother's documents indicate that they eloped to Elkton, Maryland, where they were married on May 25, 1935. Rae and I were told that they lived with my father's parents and worked side by side as beauticians in their tiny basement; however, their marriage license states that my mother was a homemaker and my father was a leather inspector. Regardless, we were told that in those days during the Depression, they would provide three treatments for a dollar—a cut, curl, and arch (eyebrow shaping), for example, or a cut, curl, and manicure. Of course, a cup of coffee in those days was five cents, so a dollar was a lot of money.

Around the beginning of World War II, my parents bought the corner house not far from Nana and Pop-Pop. Documents indicate that they had a beauty shop in this new residence and that it was licensed, as was my father. For reasons never revealed to me, my father divorced my mother and married a woman in Georgia. My mother must have been savvy enough to keep the house during the war, as she was able to find work as a beautician at Wanamaker's, an upscale department store. She bought decorations for the house as well as china and glassware at the department store, and on occasion she would buy her mother fine clothes, which she loved to do. Mom was very house-proud, a trait that rubbed off on my sister and me.

Sometime after the end of the war, having divorced his relatively new bride, my father returned to Philadelphia. He remarried my mother on April 16, 1949. I would have considered his behavior an ominous warning of things to come, but my mother must have loved my father enough to marry him again. (In fact, their marriage and subsequently our family life became so chaotic later on that Mom never discussed with me the simple pleasures of romance and marriage—not even when I got old enough to know about them. And, strangely enough, she never acknowledged Rae's or my wedding anniversary.)

It was then that my parents decided to have children and my mother underwent some gynecological manipulations. I was conceived shortly after Mom had her surgery, and I was born in December 1950. Not long after that, my parents moved to the outskirts of Philadelphia, and a few years later, they had Rae, their second and final child.

Mom did not work while Rae and I were young. She was the perfect homemaker: the floors were always scrubbed, the baseboards were always dusted—nothing was out of place. Dinner was prepared faithfully every night, always with a homemade dessert unless we had store-bought ice cream. It was always served promptly at 6:00 p.m., coinciding with my father's return from work and the time required for him to "freshen up" before appearing at his place at the kitchen table. Mom always catered to my father's tastes, preparing his favorite foods—sautéed ground beef, mashed potatoes, and peas, green beans, or corn. On Friday nights she would serve either oyster stew or flounder, and on Sundays she always prepared something special, like pot roast, chicken, or meatloaf without onions. Sometimes Mom would prepare liver, which I hated, and which filled the house with a disagreeable odor. One of my father's favorite meals during the hot summers was a platter of uncooked vegetables—including raw potatoes. He never ate anything Italian, which was unfortunate because my mother's culinary abilities were essentially held in abeyance for many years. My mother loved to bake, her specialties being pound cake, cream puffs, and *springerle*, a German Christmas cookie with anise seeds, which was one of my father's favorites.

In addition to cooking and cleaning, Mom also reared my sister and me. She potty-trained me by the time I was one year old, which is hard to imagine, and she always saw that we were nice and clean in freshly ironed outfits when our father came home at the end of the day. (Just before his arrival, my sister always seemed to lose one shoe, which my mother would rush to locate either inside or outside, depending upon the weather.) My mother, being a hairdresser, always had our hairdos just so; she would scrub our heads as she washed our hair and then pull it back tightly into perfect ponytails. As we got older, she would wash and set our hair every Saturday and give us Toni permanents when we needed them—that was not my favorite part of the week. She always wanted us to be proud of how we looked, especially how our hair was styled.

During my formative years and throughout my mother's married life, Mom did all the washing and ironing. She would wash my father's work clothes, put his pants on metal stretch hangers, and then iron them once they were dry so there would always be a sharp crease down both legs. She would also iron his khaki-colored work shirts. Every day my father wore two outfits: his work clothes and the outfit he would change into upon his arrival home from work. In those days there were no permanent-press fabrics, so everything had to be ironed, plus my father's shirts had to be hand-starched before they were ironed. Mom also ironed our dresses, choir vestments, Girl Scout and Brownie uniforms, and play outfits. She worked hard to make sure everything was just so.

Mom would take pains to serve her guests an excellent holiday meal, dressing the table with a carefully ironed linen tablecloth and clearing the floor of any stray toys Rae and I had carelessly left there. She was an eager-to-please hostess who attempted to do everything to perfection—a trait that unfortunately transferred itself to me as I got older. Sadly, my mother rarely received praise for her efforts, and I think this made her feel underappreciated, like a second-class citizen. But that's the way things were in the 1950s—a successful man was the head of his household, with a supportive, good woman standing in the shadows behind him.

In many ways we could have been considered the picture-perfect family, and in certain respects we were. But that picture began to change, and what followed had a profound effect on my life. This wonderful family turned out to be a temporary situation, and as a result I struggled most of my life with a mental illness whose roots go back to the place I always called home.

Chapter 2

My First Setback and Recovery

When I was young, I saw my father as the very loyal head of our family—a good father, devoted husband, and dependable provider. My mother was equally devoted and dependable. She was an excellent parent, an industrious housekeeper, and a truly great cook. I was very happy and thought this was the way life was supposed to be. As I grew older, however, I realized I had been living in a dream, because my life eventually took a 180-degree turn.

When I was seven years old, my family moved from our little Toll Brothers suburban house to the northeast section of Philadelphia so my father could be closer to work. Our new home was semidetached with a partially finished full-size basement. As they did with our previous house, my parents worked on this one until it was just right—a home they could be proud of.

My transfer to the large local public elementary school, which I entered as a second grader, was a big shift for me, not only in terms of size but also academically. In my suburban school, I'd never had any difficulty with reading or writing; perhaps I'd been too young to realize I had learning issues. Upon entering the second grade, however, it became crystal clear that I had *significant* issues with reading, word recognition, sounding out words, comprehension, and writing. I later came to understand that I suffered from dyslexia, which made reading impossible for a long while.

And so, along with about ten other students, I was assigned to Mrs. Noel's reading adjustment class for improvement in language arts and reading skills. Mrs. Noel proved to be very patient as she reviewed with us the sounds that each letter made and showed us how vowel sounds blended with consonants. Every day I would leave my regular classroom to spend about forty-five minutes with her, but no matter how hard I tried, I just couldn't master reading. It seemed that I was stuck in *Dick and Jane* primers for years! As a result, I hated to read. Every week, my second grade class would go to the school library to pick out new books to read, which was a total waste of time and actually gave me anxiety. I would pick out the easiest book, look at the pictures, and return it unread a week later.

By the age of seven, I was fully aware that my happy little world was turning into one of significant difficulty. Being sent to a different class because of my inability to read made me feel inferior to my classmates. This, in turn, made me feel self-conscious and stupid. (Today I wonder if I picked up this inferiority complex from my mother, who had always harbored similar feelings.) My parents, trying to soften the blow, suggested that my problem was likely related to my change from a school in the country to one in a big city. Though I bought into these excuses, the fact remained that I could not read or write.

To survive my embarrassment, I tried to buy some slack by being a good little girl and performing well in subjects like math, spelling, and citizenship. My strategy didn't work. I simply could not read, and that deficiency affected everything else, including my ability to make friends. Whenever it came time to divide the class up into teams, I was always one of the last students chosen; my classmates didn't want me on their teams because I wasn't on their intellectual level. Subsequently I withdrew socially, having realized that being a good little girl had no benefit. To compound matters, my grades at the end of the year were so poor in both reading and writing that I had to repeat the second grade. I was not off to a good start.

That summer my father and mother signed me up for paid individual tutoring at the local private day school, which was only a block away from our house. I would do the assigned work each night and then walk to the school each morning to go over the assignments with my teacher. It proved to be a beneficial decision on my parents' part, as I managed to get through second and third grade over the next two years, though I continued to leave the classroom for my daily forty-five minutes of reading adjustment with Mrs. Noel.

Fourth grade produced another set of upsetting issues. That's when the Philadelphia school system restructured its academic year. When I first entered elementary school, each grade was divided into two sections, A and B. Both sections were offered twice a year, from September through January and again from February to June. So rather than always starting school in September, a child could start first grade, 1A, in February and pick up the second half, 1B, the next September. The restructuring called for one continuous academic year, always beginning in September and ending in June. There would be no mid-year promotions.

When the restructuring occurred, I was in the 4A section that ran from February to June. My options were either to repeat the first half of fourth grade in September and then enter the second half in February or to skip the second half of fourth grade in September and go directly into fifth grade. To me, the choice was obvious: I wanted to be advanced to fifth grade.

One day near the end of my 4A session, I was called to the office of the principal, Dr. Barkley. I hurried to obey, thinking, *What have I done that's so bad that I have to go to the principal's office?* Upon my arrival, I found my mother there, which came as a total surprise, since she never came to the school except to attend parent-teacher conferences. This made me extremely apprehensive. It wasn't long before I understood what she and Dr. Barkley were discussing: my weak reading skills meant I wasn't ready to skip half a year of academic studies. But in order to be held back, I needed to be failing *three* subjects. It was therefore arbitrarily decided that I would receive failing grades in reading, language arts, and written expression. Although this decision was made in my best interest, I didn't see it that way. I cried and cried and cried. Being held back a second time was much too difficult for me to comprehend or accept, producing yet another blow to my self-esteem and making me feel like a total failure. Dr. Barkley, a tall, beautiful woman, was known to be a strict principal, but she also loved children. Sensing that I was upset, she removed her beautiful pearl bracelet with its gold-and-pearl acorn pendant and presented it to me. It was a thoughtful gesture that I never forgot, but in spite of that kindness, I remained sad and my self-confidence was further weakened.

Once again finding myself in fourth grade, I continued to go to reading adjustment classes. I was beginning to get the hang of reading, albeit very slowly and with minimal confidence, and I finally passed fourth grade and went to the next level. It was in fifth grade that I finally figured out how to read, although I remained a *very slow* reader and my comprehension was less than stellar. My perseverance and hard work paid off, and I was released from reading adjustment—hallelujah!—but for the rest of my years in school, I never managed to read at grade level.

As my ego healed, I became a happier child. Other students began to include me on their teams as I became accepted and more popular. This gave me the wings to fly that I had so longed for, and my grades began to rise as well. Now I was both a good little girl and a good student (although I still hated reading, which remained a difficult task). When I reached the sixth grade, my peers elected me class president—beneficial assurance that my school life was headed in a positive direction. In seventh grade I was elected vice-president of the student council, and I was recognized as a hard worker because of my school grades, my extracurricular activities, and a job I held in the cafeteria. I considered this a major personal victory, though achieving it had taken a painfully long time.

But the long-term effects of those early elementary school experiences had eroded my self-confidence and left me vulnerable to criticism. Making friends was still an effort for me. Despite the ideals of hard work, perseverance, and perfection that were ingrained in me, my self-esteem remained low—although I was unaware of that fact until one of my nursing instructors in college told me I had a poor self-image. Reversing a poor self-image isn't an easy process, for it tends to take hold of you for a lifetime, popping up when least expected.

Though I remain a slow reader even today, my comprehension soared. Writing became one of my passions, and I grew to love reading to my children when they were young. I still enjoy reading with my grandchildren; presently I'm in the process of helping my five-year-old granddaughter learn her letters and the sounds associated with them. Fortunately, I was able to make the best of a difficult situation through the intervention of my parents and the helpful adults I encountered during my school years. Needless to say, it was a difficult process to go through at such an early age, but it was made considerably more bearable by the love and support both my parents exhibited. Little did I know that, in the years to come, I would regard those years as the *easy* part of my life.

Chapter 3

When Life Began to Change

Change is inevitable in life, but as a child I had no idea how many changes were going to occur in mine. Of course, none of us can predict the twists and turns our lives will take, or how we will respond to them. We all go through physical, mental, and emotional changes, as well as changes within our family, our environment, and the world at large. Nothing stands still. Everything is in a state of flux and transition.

Between the ages of seven and nine, I had a fairly healthy, happy, and balanced life (despite contracting the usual childhood diseases, including chicken pox, measles, German measles, and eczema). At age nine, I felt I had been prematurely launched into adulthood in many ways—not only physically, but *practically*. The major reason I felt this way was that Mom returned to work. Up until then, I would come home from school, watch some television, have a snack, and maybe go out and play. I loved to jump rope and roller-skate (I had the kind of skates that you clipped on to the soles of your shoes and then tightened with a skate key so they wouldn't fall off). I also played hopscotch, rode my bicycle, and jumped around on my pogo stick. I was athletic but not very sociable. Making friends was not one of my strengths—largely because of the inferiority complex I had developed while doing poorly in school.

When it rained, I might play with my dollhouse, but not with much imagination. I had a Barbie doll and some outfits for her, but I tended to keep her neatly tucked away in her black Barbie case. I *did* color a lot, which I enjoyed. As I previously mentioned, my grandmother taught me how to do handiwork; making pot holders was my specialty. I was also a member of Brownie Troop 750, which met at St. John's church. With the help of the best Scout leaders in the world, I eventually rose in rank to become a senior Girl Scout. Over time I earned fifty badges and knocked on many doors, selling a lot of Girl Scout cookies so I could go on weeklong camping trips. I don't remember playing much with my mother, since she was always keeping house, cooking, baking, and chauffeuring my sister and me from place to place.

It's easier to understand in retrospect the forces that caused many of the changes in my life, but as a child I was not prepared for most of them. I thought life would go on in a relatively positive state, but that was not to be. There were physical changes, which seemed natural and which I eventually anticipated—I knew I was getting older. But I did not expect to mature into a woman at the age of nine. Fortunately, my mother knew the warning signs and features of feminine maturity, so she was able to help me through this transition. I had a significant growth spurt at that time, going from four-feet-eight to five-feet-four before I turned ten, at a weight of ninety-five pounds. I looked like a stick with big, brown eyes and long, brown hair. I gradually began to fill out. In fact, I remember my fifth-grade teacher saying something to me about needing a bra. Then I got my period, which was not totally upsetting to me; in Girl Scouts I had seen a film on maturation and the advent of menses. But nothing was as graphic as my mother's statement about this change in my life. After she had outfitted me with the necessary items, she said, "Never let any man take your pants down!" I got the message, realizing that sex was a normal part of development. I was the tallest girl in my class for several years, and also the only one who had a monthly period. By the time I reached the tenth grade, I weighed 126 pounds while still being five-feet-four.

For a couple of years I took ballet classes at the local recreation center, and I participated in a couple of recitals at the public high school close to my Philadelphia home. They were a big deal because of the costumes my Aunt Susie crafted for me and the makeup my neighbor Denise applied to my face. As a young girl, I'd sung in the junior choir at church; when I got older, I sang in the senior choir. Mrs. Fairchild, our director, was an accomplished organist, and it was she who instilled in me a love of church hymns and classical music. Meanwhile, I took organ lessons at school and learned to play the viola. Unfortunately I was defeated by the former instrument, but I became quite accomplished at the latter. In school I was exposed to both classical music and show tunes. Those days of singing in school choirs and playing in orchestras and bands (oh yes, I tooted the tuba!) continue to influence my musical tastes today.

I always did my homework after dinner. When I was a youngster, Mom would help me with my speed drills in basic math facts, listen to my oral spelling, and prepare me for social studies tests by asking me questions. Because I hated reading due to my poor skills, I always avoided any homework that required it. I must confess surprise that my parents failed to encourage me to read, since that was my true area of scholastic weakness. (Later, when my daughter had difficulty reading, we both attended a course offered by the Department of Educational Psychology at the University of Pennsylvania and Children's Hospital in Philadelphia. As part of each evening's assignment, we were required to participate in a reading activity, which helped both of us.)

Life changed when I reached my ninth year and Mom went to work. I still wanted to do the things I'd previously enjoyed, and my sister wanted to continue with *her* activities, which consisted mostly of playing with friends. Rae had a great imagination and had no trouble playing make believe with her friends. Her best friend, Nora, lived next door, so she spent a lot of time playing with her. Rae was never quite as conscientious or serious as I was about responsibilities, including housework, helping Mom, and schoolwork. She made friends easily and loved to spend lots of time with Nora, while I had few friends in the neighborhood. Although we were both in Scouts, I was more serious about earning badges and learning the ways of a true Girl Scout. Rae was less serious about that, and about life in general. Maybe it had something to do with her being a second child. As a matter of fact, Rae had a boyfriend in the first grade, and the joke in the family was that I would become a doctor and Rae would marry one—goals that neither of us would accomplish.

When Mom went to work at the beauty salon, my life changed radically. Money was tight, and Mom wanted to help out with the household expenses and pay for Rae's and my activities. Because I was the eldest child, Mom expected me to do the cleaning up. While she thought Rae should help out with the many daily chores, I was assigned the responsibility of inducing her cooperation. Though Mom would talk with Rae about helping around the house, ultimately I was the enforcer. The chores included making the beds, cleaning the bathrooms, emptying and cleaning the ashtrays (both my parents smoked a pack of unfiltered Camels a day), setting the table for dinner, and getting dinner started. After-dinner chores included washing and drying the dishes and putting them away, wiping down the kitchen table, cleaning the stove, and sweeping the floor. It seemed like a marathon of work before and after dinner, and I wasn't particularly happy about it, but verbalizing my complaints didn't go over well with my parents. I was often asked, "Who do you think you are—America's *guest?*" Mom continued to do the heavy work—cleaning the house and washing and ironing, although I *did* help fold the laundry, especially the socks and towels. But I was unable to get my sister's help with the other chores, so I ended up doing them all by myself. Consequently, Rae and I got into a lot of fights, for she saw *playing* as her job! I know now that she was right; it was unrealistic to think that she should have been able to do half the chores at age seven.

Clearly, working around the house was not a traumatic experience, but it put me in work mode most of the time. Not only did I work around the house, but I also worked at school. When I was in the fourth grade, I was asked to help out in the cafeteria after lunch. I was the only child in grades four through seven who helped in the cafeteria. I washed off all twenty-two of the lunchroom tables, returned the unsold cartons of milk to the large walk-in refrigerator, cleared the steam table, and put all the candy back on the storage shelves. Additionally, I washed all the lunch trays and silverware and was responsible for cleaning up the teachers' lunchroom and bringing their dirty dishes to the cafeteria manager, Mrs. Lansdale. I got paid two dollars a week for these tasks. Now, none of this was hard work, but it definitely cut into my playtime, which was also my time for socializing with other students. True, I earned a reputation for being a good worker, but I would like to have been able to go out on the playground with the other children—another missed life experience that I did not recognize at the time. Again, while the work itself was not traumatic, it did have a large impact on my life, leading to increased difficulty forming relationships.

After Mom had been working for a few years, things really began to change in our household. I honestly don't know exactly why, but intense battles began to erupt between my parents, and they were really scary for Rae and me. As I said earlier, Mom shouldered the bulk of the responsibility for taking care of us and maintaining the household, despite the few tasks I undertook. This is not to say my father was a slacker in any sense of the word; he continued to work, pay the bills, manage the finances, renovate the house, and repair our cars. I imagine my parents felt a certain amount of stress, rearing two children and managing the household while working full-time. It is possible that my father may have felt threatened because he wasn't the sole breadwinner in the family.

Rae and I reaped benefits from Mom's job, for she was able to buy us new clothes with her earnings. Thus our wardrobes were nice and neat but not excessive; we still wore hand-me-downs from my cousin, but most of them were handcrafted by my aunt, who worked in a high-end suit factory. Nevertheless, my father did not recognize or appreciate my mother's efforts. This, in turn, might have made her feel less romantic toward him, thus affecting their sexual relationship. This is only speculation, but my father once said to me when I was a young teenager, "The way to a man's heart is *not* through his stomach, but through his *pants!*" I understood what he meant, but looking back as an adult, I realize that he was way off-base with such a bold comment, which he never should have said to me when I was so young.

Then my father began to have an extramarital relationship, which my mother discovered by following him like a private investigator to see where he went. Since his trips always terminated at the same place, my mother began to confront him about them. She would refer to the subject of her investigations as the "whore from Alleghany." This discovery led to many loud, knock-down fights, which Rae and I witnessed. I don't know the reason for my father's affair, but I know it took place—a fact he always denied.

When my parents fought, there was screaming and swearing, as well as physical abuse of my mother by my father. My mom often had bruises from the punches my father delivered. These fights would occur nightly, always after dinner, occasionally while we were still clearing the table. Understandably, my sister and I were terrified by these frequent battles and fled to the second story of our house. There, sitting huddled together on the top step, we would listen to our parents go at it, fearful that they would get a divorce. Sometimes I was so frightened during their fights that I would sneak downstairs to the dining room, where the house's only phone was located, and call the police. Upon their arrival, they would simply tell my parents to calm down. This would put a chill in the air, and my parents would stop fighting for a while. What followed was a long period of silence between them, sometimes lasting for months. My sister and I would refer to these interludes as "the silent treatment."

My parents occasionally put my sister and me in the middle of their wars, or so I thought at the time. But now, looking back, I can see clearly that I put *myself* in the middle. I didn't like the way my father treated my mother, especially when it came to physical abuse, and so I began to side with her. If my mother did not talk to my father, I would not talk to my father. As I got older, I would counsel my mother and urge her to get a divorce, advice that she did not heed. My sister sensibly went about doing her own thing, which was playing and staying out of the disputes. She was the smart one, while I was the more involved one—not a wise move on my part. But how could I have known that?

Having sided with my mother, I began to lose respect for my father. I saw him as a mean, threatening, hateful, spiteful person. This was a 180-degree turn from having been my father's little girl. The fact that I'd taken my mother's side did not please him, so I too became an enemy. My father would beat me if I did something he disliked—including speaking to my mother in a disrespectful tone, which was perplexing, since he rarely sided with her. Once when I was outside playing jump rope after dinner, my mother called me in to do the dishes. Not knowing why she'd called, I said, "Yeah, what do you want?" My father took umbrage at this apparent disrespect, and I subsequently received a severe beating for "talking back" to my mother. He was crafty in beating me on the backs of my legs, my bottom, and my back, because no one would see the welts and bruises he left. Another time I must have done something wrong at the dinner table—frankly I don't remember what, but I remember the punishment. Whatever the misdemeanor, my father decided I should be banned from the dinner table and not be allowed to eat dinner with the family for months. I was banished to the basement, where I ate my dinner at the old kitchen table next to his workbench. I remember how hurt I felt, and even today I wonder how bad my behavior could have been to deserve such a punishment.

An even greater mystery is why my mother didn't come to my defense. Was she paralyzed and unable to stand up to my father? After all, I had stood up for *her* and took her side when my father was mean to her. Before Mom died in 2008, I asked her if she remembered my being banished to the basement. But she had no memory of such an event. My mother never suffered from Alzheimer's, but perhaps her pain and misery superseded mine to such a degree that she automatically erased the incident from her memory.

As I got older, I worked hard to curry favor with both my parents. As hard work was a well-regarded hallmark of our family, on Saturdays I would often clean my neighbor's house for eight dollars, and I would detail cars for a dollar, a bargain that my family and neighbors cashed in on. I also babysat for three different families. The McCarthy family had five children under the age of five, and I would babysit them for fifty cents an hour—and seventy-five cents an hour after midnight. I also cleaned for the McCarthys periodically throughout the year, and during summer vacation I would iron basketfuls of their shirts and baby clothes. My parents were amenable to my working for this large Irish Catholic family. To say I worked hard for my money is an understatement!

Next to the McCarthys lived a lovely family with only two children. The mother was an elementary school teacher, and the father was a lawyer. I received the same wages from them as from the McCarthys, even though the workload was less. However, since there were only two children and their mother was off from school during the summer months, they had less need for a babysitter.

Another family with two children lived two doors down from our house. The husband, a steward on a merchant marine ship, was away at sea most of the time, so the mother, "Jane," needed extra assistance. My mother and Jane had formed a friendship; they often chatted and had a cup of coffee together. My mother had no objection to my babysitting Jane's two children, and I liked the work because I got a dollar an hour with less to do. My father, however, did not like Jane and objected to me babysitting for her because he suspected her of having extramarital relationships—a clear example of the pot calling the kettle black. One night, as I was about to leave our house to sit with Jane's children, my mother and father had a huge argument about my babysitting. The volume and pitch finally took their toll on me, as I perceived myself as being the source of the dispute. As the battle gained in intensity, I panicked. I ran outside and hid under the weeping willow tree in our backyard, where I cried and screamed inconsolably. Bent over in a fetal position with my hands clapped over my ears, I rocked back and forth, unable to tolerate the screaming that emanated from my house. Little did I realize that, at the age of twelve, I was having my first panic attack. Part of my anxiety came from my father's accusations that I was not listening to him, that I was doing what I "damn well pleased." Eventually my mother came out and held me lovingly, trying to soothe me, and I calmed down. I can't remember if I babysat that night, but I suspect I didn't, for I was terribly upset. In spite of what happened that night, I continued to babysit for Jane with the support of my mother. I lost favor with my father, however.

My father did give me two very nice presents, even when I was on the outs with him, but they came at a price—and I don't mean money. When I was in the eighth grade, I would type up my science notes on my father's elite typewriter. It was large, black, and very heavy. That winter, around the time of my birthday, I woke up one morning to find an early birthday present sitting next to my father's typewriter. It was a gray portable typewriter with pica font; it came in a lightweight gray case. I was thrilled until I read the note affixed to it: "Remember, it is not the keys that make the mistakes, but rather the person who pushes the keys." His message was clear: I was messing up. So although I was happy with the gift, I felt I had again done something wrong. In my mind, the note minimized the good my father had done for me.

He gave me the other gift when I was sixteen. By then my father and I had not spoken much in several years. He paid little attention to me, regardless of what I was doing—which was largely attending school and being involved in school activities. But for my birthday that year, he gave me a one-quarter-carat, princess-cut diamond ring in a platinum setting. Although it was a very nice sixteenth birthday gift, there was no card, nothing written, attached to it. I should have been grateful, but in all honesty I kept thinking, *Why do I need a diamond ring? This looks like an engagement ring!* I would rather have had a hug and a kiss and some acknowledgment that I was a decent human being—but those things never came. I found my father's random acts of kindness hurtful, and they made me sad. I hardly ever wore the ring.

I was also upset by my father's hurtful acts toward my mother. When she was upset, it tended to distress me. One time, my father took the beautiful china dishes my mother had worked so hard to buy during the war and threw them into a waste dump, saying that she loved *things* more than she loved *him*. There probably was a lot of truth to that—but then again, who could love such a brutal and evil person? My mother was proud of the dishes and crystal that she had managed to put together when my father was romancing another woman during World War II. This act of cruelty on his part simply forced her to save for another, smaller set of china.

Another spiteful thing my father did was take my mother's new washer and dryer, which she had purchased with the money she earned working as a hairstylist in the early 1960s and give them to his girlfriend the so-called "whore from Alleghany." His explanation: she needed them more than my mother did. His cruelty was inexplicable. He expected my mother to do his laundry but took away her tools to do the job. My mother was heartbroken and outraged; his action was the impetus of World War III in our household. But my mother was a strong woman, and she worked to get another set of machines, which my father had no reason to confiscate.

Though my father often victimized my mother, she never retaliated physically. She fought back verbally, but unlike him, she never resorted to violence. Her only physical retaliation against him was her eventual refusal to sleep in the same room with him. Consequently, my parents lived separate lives in the same household—a relationship without any beauty or love.

These incidents didn't just affect my mother; they also damaged my sister and me. Today I still can't say whether it should be a child's responsibility to side with one parent against the other, since that only results in the child getting the short end of the stick, unloved by the un-championed parent; I believe that my sister was wise to remain neutral. Nevertheless, for me, our parents' battles were both traumatic and unsettling. I had never expected to be part of such a dysfunctional household. In addition to having a poor self-image due my to academic issues, I was now struggling with intense emotional fear and animosity. Not only had I lost the love of a parent to whom I had been very close, but I also had been physically and emotionally beaten by that same "loving" parent. I remember having these intense feelings and not knowing what to do about them. I once spoke with Father King, the rector of the church I attended in the Holmesburg section of Philadelphia, telling him how upset I was about the way my parents were always cursing, but I was so distressed that I could not find the right words to accurately describe what was going on in our family. To his credit, he made a home visit, but it didn't make any impact on my parents' relationship.

I often begged my mother to get a divorce, but her reply was always the same: "I'm staying with your father for you kids." This usually prompted me to ask, "For what purpose?" After all, we were living in a chaotic household where the tension was so thick you could cut it with a knife. I think the real reason Mom was reluctant to leave him was that she couldn't afford to take care of two kids and herself without his financial support. I hated being a part of this family that, as a small girl, I had so adored. As I grew older, I was determined never to stay married to a man who laid a hand on me. Nor would I carry on in front of *my* children the way my parents did in front of Rae and me. By the time I was eleven, I was growing more and more emotionally fragile.

A few years later, another significant event impacted my life. Three things that Mom's family—her brothers and sisters and our cousins—loved to do were eating, swimming, and talking to each other. So they would regularly go to my aunt's and uncle's home to have potluck barbeques and swim in their pool. As a result, Mom's side of the family remained very close. My aunt and uncle gladly took Rae and me into their home when my parents had an evening engagement. We would show up in time for dinner with the family and then spend the evening with my aunt and uncle until my parents returned to pick us up.

Sometimes when I was visiting, my uncle would ask me if I'd like to ride down to the bakery with him. I saw no reason to decline, for we were all part of a loving family and not strangers to each other. On those occasions I would wait in the parked car while he went into the bakery; after a few minutes he would return with his purchase of goodies. Over time, this became an enjoyable routine. Then one night, when I was fourteen, my uncle returned to the car and didn't drive directly home. Instead, he leaned over and started kissing me with increasing passion, fondling my breasts and rubbing my belly. He did this for ten to fifteen minutes before returning home, warning me to tell no one about the interlude. This happened repeatedly. Being incredibly sheltered and ignorant about that sort of behavior, and being in want of affection, I reasoned that it was okay because he had never attempted to remove my panties, which was all my mother had warned me about. But surprisingly, after several such incidents had occurred over the years, something inside me rebelled, and I said, "Stop!" Fortunately he did, and I never went to the bakery with him again.

I'm not quite sure what prompted me to put a halt to my uncle's behavior, but a little voice inside me whispered that it was wrong. Nevertheless, I honored his request and never told a soul. Then one day when I was hospitalized as an adult, I was in group therapy discussing sexual abuse and a light went on in my head: my uncle's behavior had been not only inappropriate, but totally wrong! Not until then had I intellectually recognized my uncle's behavior as a betrayal of my innocence—and even then, I did not process the ramifications of the experience.

Then in the 1990s, my psychiatrist at the time, Dr. Ulrich, recommended a workbook on sexual abuse. She told me not to read the entire book in one weekend; she didn't want me to fall apart, which was a strong possibility, for I was quite emotionally fragile at that time. One advantage of having had such an experience was that, as both a mother and a teacher, I've been able to share the importance of warning children about sexual abuse, and the importance of victims being able to share the resulting scars with someone who believes them. Many adults who have been sexually abused as children try to share this information with someone else, only to find that they are not believed. This is a sad situation that places the victim in a vulnerable position of mistrust.

A couple of years later, in a session with my therapist, Dr. Williams, I finally realized the impact of my uncle's violation of the naive girl I had once been. The realization was so shocking that after my session I went home and straight to bed. I lay there, curled up in the fetal position, crying and moaning uncontrollably for hours, as though my heart had been broken. When my husband, Arthur, arrived home, I was still in bad shape. With great difficulty, I shared with him for the first time my memories of the abuse. Although he tried to comfort me, I was inconsolable, and so he called Dr. Williams, who recommended we go out to dinner and then go someplace that I would enjoy. I slowly put myself together and ventured out, clinging to Arthur's arm, wanting to be as close to him as possible. If I could have, I would have crawled *inside* him to be protected. Fortunately, Arthur understood that my uncle's behavior was not my fault, and he understood my intense feelings of being violated. That night we went to a local diner, but I found that I could hardly eat. After dinner, however, we went to a garden center and walked around, which was very lovely and therapeutic for me. Upon returning home, we went straight to bed, where we clung to each other until I fell asleep. Although the cause of my emotional desperation had occurred years earlier, and although I had not been in touch with my uncle for a long time, I still needed the comfort of Arthur's closeness and protection. The following morning, which was a Saturday, Dr. Williams called to check on me, offering to see me that day if necessary. Thankfully, I was much improved.

When I arrived at my next session, Dr. Williams suggested I write my uncle a letter, which I could either mail or burn. So I wrote him a long letter explaining that I now understood how his sexual advances had violated an innocent child who now, as a grown woman, had to live an irreparably damaged life. I also shared with him my deep feelings of hurt because he crossed the line with me. I addressed the letter to him and his wife, but ultimately I chose to burn it, not wishing to cause any more trouble in our family.

Life, with all its variables, is complicated. It changes without warning, and we have no idea what lies ahead or how we'll respond to it. As children we mirror the behaviors of those around us, and the lessons and behaviors we learn ultimately become our core values, right or wrong. Reality and life experiences tell us that many of these values are neither healthy nor helpful; however, they remain ingrained in us for life, and consequently they are extremely difficult to undo. It is amazing to see how these core values can reappear, even after years of working so hard to banish them. The seeds planted in our brains early in life take strong root and are difficult to dig out, cut down, or completely eliminate.

Chapter 4

Moving to Delaware and the Death of My Father

*P*eople tend to hope that if they move, their lives will change for the better. This is often untrue. In reality, people take their problems with them, and sometimes those problems are compounded by the move itself. In the summer of 1966, when I was fifteen years old and about to enter the tenth grade, the Philadelphia company where my father had worked for many years closed down. Because he was highly skilled in the business of tanning leather, he found a job at a tannery in Wilmington, Delaware, where he became a well-regarded employee.

My parents sold their house in Philadelphia and bought a semidetached corner house on the outskirts of Wilmington, near the boundary separating the city from the town of Greenville, which was considered a rather exclusive Delaware location. Mom sewed new drapes for the windows, but they were the only cosmetic change she could afford to make to the house. My father went to work as usual, but she could only get a job as an assistant hairstylist. (In Pennsylvania, she had been grandfathered in as a master stylist due to her many years of experience. However, in Delaware there was no reciprocity for her work as a hairstylist in Pennsylvania.) It goes without saying that as an assistant, Mom could not make as much money as she did before, despite working in an exclusive shop in Greenville. Nevertheless, she maintained a financial contribution to the house and to our family.

The fighting, the physical beatings, and the terrible silences that followed continued. Mom regularly went to a Catholic church in Wilmington, where she would make novenas to give her the strength to see life through, and pray that she would never be a financial burden on her children. God answered both her petitions. To make a novena, Mom would go to church for nine days in a row, usually saying the rosary and praying to Saint Anthony to intercede on her behalf. I accompanied her a few times but didn't follow her religious path while I was in high school. (I continued with the Episcopal tradition and then went to the local Baptist church.) My father never went to church, but he did frequently go to Philadelphia to see his father—and possibly his girlfriend.

Although there were four small bedrooms in our house, my father decided to sleep in the large, partially finished attic. Even though it got very hot in the summer—the house didn't have any air-conditioning— he remained isolated up there with just a small fan for cooling. At that point we were all going in different directions, and the appearance of family life was barely maintained. My father continued to shell out $35 from his $125 weekly paycheck for food for the family, but he no longer did any household maintenance. My mother continued cooking the meals and taking care of the laundry and the house, with some assistance from me. Meanwhile, my sister went to school and basically continued doing what she enjoyed doing with her many new friends.

In September 1966, I entered the tenth grade not knowing a soul. Making new friends was challenging for me, because most of the other students had been attending Wilmington schools for the past decade and had established their respective social circles. My teachers, however, were great, especially my English teacher, Bruce Laddie.

Quite by accident, I got involved with the drama department through playing the viola in the orchestra. The first viola player, Jeffrey, was the costume master for the school plays. He was working on the musical *Little Me*, and he asked me if I knew how to sew. When I told him I did, he assigned me the job of beading a red brocaded gown. Since it was an intricate, time-consuming job, I worked on it every spare minute I had, and my mother helped me too. I was also assigned to create several other costumes for *Little Me*. After Jeffrey graduated at the end of that school year, I took over as costume mistress for the drama department.

Mr. Laddie, my English teacher, was a true gentleman—extremely upright and very talented. He had written several musicals and dramas, could play the piano, and also designed magnificent sets for our plays, with scenery that looked like it could have come straight from Broadway. The next play I remember doing was *The Miracle Worker*. Although I did not have an acting part in the play, I showed up every morning for rehearsal. At some point Mr. Laddie asked me to stage the fight scene between Annie Sullivan and Helen Keller. The directions in the script were very clear, and we had to make this extended, rather violent scene look real. Both actresses did amazing work, following the script to the letter. I was also responsible for making the costumes, which were ready in time for the dress rehearsal, but not a day earlier. The biggest problem I had was that the actors' makeup rubbed off on the cotton costumes, so every night of the play I had to wash and iron each one. I also helped Mr. Laddie with the programs and had them printed. *The Miracle Worker* was a great first experience in serious drama, and I made several friends while participating in these school productions. I also benefited from being at school most of the time, away from my family dynamics and dysfunction.

Mr. Laddie and his wonderful wife, Ruth, took me under their wings. I don't remember telling them about my chaotic household, but I suppose they were a part of God's plan to look out for me. Both Mr.

and Mrs. Laddie were very religious, and at the time I was seeking a deeper religious experience. The Laddies attended a Baptist church just a few blocks from my house, so they invited me to go with them. The teachings of Reverend Miller were amazing, and I liked the enthusiasm and friendliness of the congregation. It was just what I needed at that time in my life.

During my junior year of high school, we did *The Sound of Music*, which was a huge production, with a large cast of characters and a total of 120 costumes that needed to be crafted. There were seven children in the Von Trapp family, and each of them had at *least* three costume changes: the clothes Maria made from curtains, their travel outfits, and their sailor uniforms. There was also Maria's wedding gown, plus costumes for approximately thirty nuns and postulates. I actually went to the local convent to find out how to make their costumes. The nuns at the parish church my mother attended were very helpful in showing me how to make both types of habits. One of the girls in the cast, who was actually Jewish but was portraying a nun in the play, took a walk outside my home wearing her habit, and a passerby said, "Good morning, Sister!"—so I knew I had done a good job on *that* costume! However, I didn't have a reliable crew to make the balance of the costumes. Furthermore, the school's home economics department apparently never involved its girls in the practical experience of sewing costumes for school plays, and it never occurred to me to ask for their help. I even cut school one day—something I had never done—and worked around the clock. The week before the play, I worked right up to dress rehearsal, sleeping less than an hour a night. As I had with prior musicals, I also played in the orchestra, so my work wasn't done until the show was over. And although it probably wasn't the best thing for my stress level (something I knew nothing about at the time), I hosted the cast party for the nearly one hundred participants involved in the production—an event that turned out to be both successful and a lot of fun.

This was a good example of my inability to say no. The word was simply not part of my vocabulary. I trace this quality back to my childhood, when I was not permitted to say, "No, I don't want to do that," without retaliation from my parents. Fortunately, my mother was very supportive; she helped me with a lot of the party preparations as well as the handiwork that went into the costumes. I was very thankful for all her assistance. She truly understood the stress I was under.

Unfortunately, not long afterward, I had two episodes of hyperventilation stemming from sheer exhaustion. About two weeks after the completion of the play, I was sitting in church and started hyperventilating. The same thing happened the following week. On both occasions I ended up in the emergency room, where my mother was advised that the event was stress-induced and that I should see a psychiatrist.

Following the doctor's orders, Mom took me to a local psychiatrist. Predicting that I would work myself to the bone again, the doctor dismissed me after that initial visit; he knew there was little hope of changing my mind. I was a classic seventeen-year-old—a stubborn girl who knew it all—and I believed it was my responsibility to make sure all the costumes were completed. I wasn't arrogant, but I possessed an exceedingly strong sense of responsibility and set high expectations for myself. My parents had instilled in me the importance of working hard and fulfilling my duties. Fortunately, I never had to do that much work again, nor did I ever hyperventilate again, though it took me awhile to de-stress and get back on track.

During my senior year, I noticed that my father was stumbling and couldn't walk in a straight line. We didn't realize at the time that he was suffering from double vision, but he must have gone to the doctor for it, because he started wearing a patch over one eye. I felt sorry for him, but we were not on speaking terms, and the doctor had no idea what was wrong with him. CAT scans and MRIs didn't exist in those days. These changes occurred in February 1968; by October 1968, my father had succumbed to a malignant brain tumor. It wasn't until many years later that I learned, as a neuro-oncology nurse, that the chemicals from the vats of dye my father worked with all his adult life were probably the cause of his brain tumor. Had my mother known this at the time, she might have been able to initiate a lawsuit. Toward the end of his life, I rarely saw my father because I was in high school in Delaware and he was in Jefferson Hospital in Philadelphia. However, I *do* remember the doctors drilling Burr holes into my father's skull to relieve the cerebral pressure. He died of a heart attack within days of that procedure.

Despite the hell my father put my mother through during their married life, she was a dutiful wife and loyal nurse during his terminal illness. Consequently, she was in Philadelphia at my father's bedside when he died. She felt comfortable contacting the Laddies and asking them to break the news to Rae and me. When they came to the house and told us about our father's death, I knew I should cry, but no tears came. Instead I thought, *Thank God he died. Now life will be more peaceful.* Nine years of trauma and abuse had been enough—but I did not realize the toll those nine years of hell would take on my life in the future. When I think today of the pain my parents imposed on my sister and me, I feel angry. Their inability to resolve their issues or their anger produced unhealthy consequences in their lives and our lives too. However, I am inclined to blame my father more than my mother.

On the day after the traditional viewing, Dad was given both military and Masonic honors at his funeral. His illness had caused him to lose twenty-five pounds—so much weight that, even with the undertaker's cosmetic skills, he looked skeletal. Following the funeral service, he was buried next to his mother in one of the three plots my grandparents had purchased at Forest Hills Cemetery outside Philadelphia.

That Christmas of 1968, the Laddies made certain that Mom, Rae, and I had a happy holiday. On Christmas Eve, they gave us presents with funny little poems and messages attached. My mother made dinner the next day for our grandfather; my aunt Evelyn and cousins Har, Karl, and Michael; and my sister and me. In spite of the loss of our father, or perhaps *because* of his passing, this was our first happy Christmas in years.

Not until much later in life did I discover that my father had named *his* father as the beneficiary of his life insurance policy, leaving nothing to his wife and children. Understandably, the death of my father was hardest on my grandfather, for his son had preceded him in death, which is not the natural order of things. Still, my mother, quite naturally, was stunned, and was forced to beg my grandfather for the money from the policy, since her hairdressing job did not provide sufficient funds for her to maintain a house and care for two daughters. My grandfather eventually gave in to my mother's pleas after much persuading. It turned out he had his own nest egg that would not only see him through the rest of his life, but would also see my mother through the rest of hers.

In June 1969, I graduated from high school with honors, having been accepted into the National Honor Society. Though not first or second in my class, I did well enough to be accepted at the University of Delaware. I definitely had come a long way from my earlier years in school. I was under no illusion, however, that my mother would pay for my college tuition or provide any financial support. I was the one who wanted to go to college, and it was clear that I would have to work my way through those years. So I secured a partial scholarship through a work-study program.

One week after my high school graduation, my mother and sister moved back to Philadelphia, into a small row house on Borbeck Street. From that moment on, I was on my own. I had learned the meaning of hard work, was not afraid of it, and was mature enough to be independent. I immediately started taking summer courses at the university. While I had developed good study habits, I quickly learned that college was a lot different and much more difficult than high school.

Meanwhile, my sister got a job at Rite Aid and subsequently graduated from Lincoln High School in Philadelphia. After graduating, she got married (I made her wedding gown), but unfortunately her marriage failed, and she was granted a divorce after eight years. I really didn't see much of my sister except when I would come home for a holiday or during the summer. She was always busy trying to work and have a child. My sister had learned the art of working very hard. She was (and is) an artist in her own right, organizing flowers for weddings, catering themed parties, and working for a caterer. During these years, Rae and I did not have a very close relationship—a carryover from our younger years.

Some life changes—like the death of my father—I was happy about. I was grateful for the Laddies, whom God had provided for me during difficult times in high school and at home. My completion of high school and my mother's move to Philadelphia were additional turning points in my life. I was again launched into adulthood, but I felt ready for it this time. I never did live at home again; I only stayed there during summer vacations and the period prior to my wedding. I was on my own, providing for myself financially and emotionally at the age of eighteen. (In those days, I suppose, this was no big deal; many girls were married and/or had full-time jobs at that age.) Attending college was difficult for me, not only because of the academic work, but also because my mother depended on me for emotional support. She had severe arthritis and did not know what to do about it. Although I repeatedly suggested she have her hip replaced, she suffered for years before doing so.

I had thought that life would be better now that my father was out of the picture, but there was more in store for me. Though I *felt* like I'd made a successful launch into adulthood, I had much to learn—key points about life I would have to learn the hard way. One of the important lessons I had totally missed while I was in high school was that I couldn't burn the candle at both ends, no matter how strong

I thought I was. I also missed the lesson that stubbornness is not necessarily a good value. I had never learned to say no when asked to do something that I really didn't want to do or have time to complete. Though I *felt* like I'd made a successful launch into adulthood, I had much to learn.

Chapter 5

College Life, Friends, Religion, and a New Family

When I started taking courses at the University of Delaware in the summer of 1969, my goal was to become a pediatrician, but I knew I didn't have the money to go to medical school. Nevertheless, having received a work-study scholarship, I took four courses that summer: one in basic college math, one in history, and two in English. I didn't do very well; I received one B and three Cs. Although I studied very hard, school was difficult for me. However, that didn't dissuade me from my lofty goal.

After returning from my morning university classes, I worked as a seamstress in the shop of a friend's parents. Susan and I had become very good friends in high school, in part because we both enjoyed sewing and playing tennis. Susan's family often invited me to the beach with them to go clamming. Now we both attended morning classes at the university. When my mother moved back to Philadelphia, Susan's family kindly invited me to work in their shop and live in their sparsely furnished extra bedroom.

Though Susan seemed much more intelligent than me, I never felt like I was competing with her. She could also sew much more quickly than I could, and since she could alter garments more rapidly, she earned more money than I did. Part of the money I earned in the dress shop went to room and board, and I used the rest for travel to and from the university and for living expenses. I was also able to save some money for the next semester of school.

Shortly after I moved in with Susan's family, I became aware that Susan was letting Brendan, her boyfriend from high school, in through the shop door around 3:00 a.m. They would come up the back stairs, go through my room, and have sex in Susan's room. This happened on a regular basis, which upset me in part because I was a prude and very religious. Incredibly, this was my first exposure to teenage sex, and I still had a lot to learn. (Strangely, the relationship I'd had with my uncle still didn't strike me as sexual in nature!) It seemed to me that their behavior was disrespectful to Susan's parents and intrusive to me, since they went through my bedroom to get to hers. In retrospect, I realize that I was judging their behavior and should have minded my own business, but at the time I told Susan quite frankly how I felt—which was unusual since I rarely voiced my disagreements about anything. After Susan confirmed my suspicions, I promised her that I would never tell her parents. But as I was uncomfortable in that situation, I decided to look for another place to live.

The church secretary had a neighbor willing to rent out a very nice spare room in her lovely home for only fifty dollars a week, and so I moved out of Susan's parents' home and into my new living quarters, feeling much more comfortable in those surroundings. I never divulged to Susan's parents the reason for my move, though they eventually discovered what had been going on. However, I continued working in their shop as a seamstress, earning enough money to pay for room and board in my new home and save money for college. Understandably, my friendship with Susan came to an end. I don't even remember running into her on campus after that.

I continued to take between fifteen and twenty-one credit hours a semester, determined to complete my bachelor's degree early. I didn't want to spend four or five years on premed courses; instead, my plan was to graduate and then work as a nurse to earn enough money for medical school. However, my lofty aspirations didn't serve me well. I suppose there are good reasons to spend the recommended four years in college and not be an overachiever and try to finish early. In fact, at that time there were a lot of students taking four and a half or five years to earn a bachelor's degree. It never occurred to me to consult a guidance counselor, which might have been a wise thing to do— although even if I had, I'm sure I would have continued to do things my way, following the established curriculum for premed and nursing. Following these guidelines took the guesswork out of determining what courses I needed to take. My greatest challenge was enrolling in courses before they filled up.

As I look back on my time in college, I can see that money (or my lack thereof) was a driving force behind all my decisions. No one else was going to take care of my finances, so I had to concern myself with this aspect of school and life in general. I worked in the cafeteria as part of my work-study program, which provided me with some additional income. Occasionally, my mother would send me a care package of soup, tea, a lovely letter, a decorative and nicely scented candle, and maybe twenty dollars, for which I was very grateful, since I realized this was a lot of money for her to contribute.

During the second semester of my freshman year, I took a basic-skills nursing course, which prepared me to be a nurse's aide. The following summer of 1970, I lived with my mother in her new house and worked at a large nursing home in Philadelphia, and at Gino's (McDonald's competition in those days) flipping burgers and waiting on customers. All told, I worked approximately eighty hours a week—shift work no less—leaving one job just in time to go home and change into my uniform for the next. My mother was a wonderful help; she always had a clean, pressed uniform ready so I would be on time for the next job. By the end of the summer, I had earned enough money to return to college, but at the expense of being absolutely exhausted. I rarely had a full day off between the two jobs, much less a short vacation. There was no one to advise me to slow down a little. My mother had never finished high school, my father was deceased, and only four people on the maternal side of my large extended family had attended college—my cousins Karl, Mike, and Har, and me, the only girl. And only Har, who had gone to college and then on to law school, had experienced similar financial and family issues. In fact, he had been working since the age of thirteen, earning money to help support his family. This was done in the name of necessity and hard work, a family trait that had been ingrained in most of us.

In September 1970, I returned to college for my sophomore year totally exhausted, but not realizing how tired I was from working so hard during the summer. That first semester I took fifteen credit hours, including organic chemistry—a science course I truly loved because it was logical and made sense to me. I went into my finals with a 4.0 average in all my courses, which pleased me; I had finally gotten the hang of college work. Then, to my surprise, the bottom dropped out of my mood and I became severely depressed. As I had no idea why, I didn't know what to do about it. (Much later in life, when I was an adult, Dr. Williams told me he suspected I had been depressed since the age of twelve.) These thoughts and feelings of depression were unfamiliar to me. At the end of the semester, I fortunately was able to complete my organic paper, but despite studying hard for all my finals, I could not remember any of the information I needed to pass them.

Inexplicably sad, with no interest in anything, I felt extremely fatigued, had no appetite, and wanted to isolate myself—all of which are symptoms of depression. I could barely eat, and none of my studying was paying off in good grades. Besides, I had no time to have fun or enjoy anything when all I did was work or study. (I still worked in the cafeteria, and I also worked weekends at the medical center, where the pay was great—about eight dollars an hour.) Fortunately, I had done well earlier in the semester, and those good grades prevented me from failing out of college. But I had blown my finals, and my semester average of 4.0 dropped to a 2.35. My overall grade point average depressed me even further, putting me in a deeper psychological hole. All my hard work had failed to pay off. Of course, maintaining a complex schedule between work and a full course load was probably the *cause* of all my problems, but I failed to see this at the time. (Later in life my husband would say, "When you are up to your ass in alligators, it's hard to remember that your mission was to drain the swamp.")

Because I'd crashed academically, my faith in God began to dwindle; I suppose I had to blame someone for my misfortune. Why would He let this happen to me? After all, I saw myself as a good person. I loved God and religiously followed his Word. (I didn't learn until I was an adult that I needed to care for and love myself as well as others.) I thought I had done my part in terms of studying and working hard. I had never been depressed before (that I was aware of). Stressed, yes; hyperventilated twice, yes; traumatized as a child, yes—but the last had occurred a long time ago. Why was the depression exhibiting itself now? And from where did it originate? Instinctively, I knew my feelings of sadness, loss of concentration, difficulty remembering, lack of interest, and desire to isolate myself were symptoms of depression. But I kept these feelings buried inside me. I failed to seek either professional psychological help or spiritual help from my friends. It seemed important to me to keep on going as if nothing in my life had changed. I was ashamed that I was depressed and angry at God.

After bombing out the first semester of my sophomore year, I "threw out the baby with the bathwater," in the words of one of my doctoral student friends at the university. I thought there was no hope of my going to medical school, considering my awful grade point average. Impulsively, I changed my major to elementary education. After all, the popular saying around campus at the time was "Those who can't do, teach."

The depression continued into second semester, but still I didn't seek help because I didn't know there was any available. Furthermore, I was embarrassed by my grades and my depression. I wasn't suicidal, but the depression caused me to spiral downward further and make impractical decisions. Not knowing any better, I continued to push on with a heavy course schedule rather than lightening my load, signing up for seventeen credit hours the following semester. Of the six courses I took, four were part of the elementary education track. These courses were supposed to be "a piece of cake"—a label I soon found to be untrue. I finished the semester with five Cs and one B, which further reduced my cumulative average to a meager 2.31!

As my depression deepened, I read quite a few philosophical books, many of which refuted the existence of God. I became absolutely certain that no loving God would allow this depression to happen to me. I was well acquainted with the biblical story of Job, and I knew he had one hell of a time despite his obedience to and faith in God. I also knew that God the Father had allowed his son, Jesus, to be crucified. But why was God allowing this to happen to *me*? I thought that depression was something I should be immune to because I was a good person and was working hard to be a caregiving professional. I even had aspirations to become a medical missionary. (Now, many years later, I see that this was God's plan for me. Yes, bad things happen to good people.)

My faith steadily dwindled to the point that I began thinking of myself as an agnostic. There was just one problem: all my friends were born-again Christians. So in addition to trying to hide my depression, I was trying desperately to conceal my agnostic thinking, continuing to associate with my friends and go to church with them. I think I did a good job of acting as though nothing was wrong. No one said anything to me about being sad, and I kept my mouth shut regarding my agnosticism, which wasn't always easy to do.

I belonged to an interfaith group that met on Tuesday nights. We would sing and pray, and Reverend Miller, the pastor of the Laddies' Baptist church in Wilmington, would come down to the university and talk and pray with us. Reverend Miller was very devoted to the group, which numbered about forty from the university. Many of us also attended his church in Wilmington; Lawrence Price, the father of George Price, a member of the group, would drive down from Wilmington to pick us up for Reverend Miller's service and then drive us back to campus after the Sunday-night prayer service.

One of the best things that happened to me early in my college days was God's intervention by giving me a family of guardian angels (my grandmother, Nana, having been my first). He had been watching over me all along, although I was unaware of it at that time. The poem "Footprints in the Sand," about faith and perseverance, has genuinely played out through my entire life, although I did not realize it until I came into "the light."

While in college, I was blessed with an entire family who watched over me and prayed for me. The Price family was very much involved in the Baptist church I attended. Their oldest son, George, also went to the university and was part of my Tuesday-night group. George and his parents, Arthur and Glenda, sang in the church choir as well. The family was very spiritual, and they loved to sing and were very talented. They were an amazing family, one I felt comfortable with and wanted to emulate. I grew very close to them and eventually began calling Arthur "Dad" and Glenda "Mom." The four Price boys considered me their sister, and even though Mom and Dad have passed on now, I remain a member of their family. They were the family I wished I'd had as a child, due to their deep love of one another, their respect for one another, and their inclusion of outsiders into their large family. They exuded a sense of peace and love for mankind and a profound love for God. Though I hadn't been *born* into their family, I was *spiritually adopted* by them. This has remained a wonderful blessing.

The summer after my sophomore year, I had an opportunity to work at Teen Challenge in the Bedford-Stuyvesant section of Brooklyn. At that time, the early 1970s, it was a notoriously poor, dangerous, drug-infested section of the borough. Teen Challenge is a drug rehabilitation center predicated on accepting Jesus and allowing Him to work in your life to rid yourself of drug addiction. Dr. Dave Wilkerson, a pastor, founded Teen Challenge and wrote the book *The Cross and the Switchblade,* which accurately describes what drug addicts go through and what the program at Teen Challenge is all about. There are presently more than two hundred Teen Challenge centers throughout the United States. Mr. and Mrs. Collins, a couple who attended the same Baptist church I did and had worked at Teen Challenge, asked my friend Tam and me if we would like to work there during the summer. Our responsibilities would include answering correspondence (letters were sometimes sent to them from jail), participating in street work (handing out religious tracts), and talking to people who frequented the Greenwich Village coffeehouse that Teen Challenge ran. Despite my agnostic stance, I accepted the offer because I could "talk the talk." This was an eye-opening experience for me, seeing the lifestyle of drug addicts. It was both illuminating and sad to see what heroin addiction did to the minds and bodies of people who habitually mainlined. The center was very helpful to those who made their best effort to detoxify and get on the right track.

I worked there the entire summer and gained a ton of weight because our diet frequently consisted of beans, rice, and potatoes. (This diet was good for the addicts, for they were often thin and unhealthy due to their drug use.) Fortunately, this job had downtime, so I was not exhausted the way I had been the previous summer, when I was working two jobs. Though my mood was still somewhat down, I felt I was getting slightly better. I think the wonderful group of people I worked with was helping me. I was also no longer isolating myself.

Another notable thing that had taken place the second semester of my sophomore year was that I became attracted to a guy named Chris, a friend of Tam's. Tall with dark, straight hair, Chris was a gentle soul who was also kind and wonderful. Though he lived in his parents' tiny old farmhouse in Newark, he would join our group on Tuesday nights. After studying, Chris and I would go for walks outside, holding hands while he whispered sweet nothings in my ear. We also talked on the phone regularly after studying. Then one night he failed to appear in our small study group, and when he didn't call me either, I anxiously began to wonder what was happening. After a few nights passed, Chris finally called to say that he was gay. I had to do some quick thinking, as this was another new experience: I had never thought about homosexuality before. I quickly responded that I still loved him as a person, that his being gay did not affect us, and that, although we could not be girlfriend and boyfriend, we could still be friends. And so we became *close* friends, not only while we were in college, but afterward too. I also became very close to Chris's family, who often had me over for dinner at their tiny homestead. During the summers, Chris and I would have popcorn and tea by candlelight at his kitchen table. (Chris's family did not have air-conditioning, and so keeping the light off made the room cooler.) During those times we spoke of many things, including our issues with faith and our mutual feelings of sadness, often talking until the wee hours of the morning.

Chris was an excellent student and ultimately became a medical librarian. He would also help me by typing my nursing papers. (One paper was ninety pages long. My teacher, Miss J., a graduate of Massachusetts General Hospital who taught medical-surgical nursing at the university, commented, "The paper was thorough but a bit too lengthy!") In addition, Chris liked to do handiwork. He made me a couple of crewel pillows as well as a cross-stitch piece that I still have to this day. In return, I made him several garments he asked for, including some caftans and a blue velvet jacket.

When I was a junior in college, Chris tried to commit suicide two or three times. My friend Tam and I visited him in the hospital. Both of us were distressed that he had attempted to take his own life, and the events had a particularly profound and lasting effect on me. Chris and I made a pact that if he ever again felt the urge to commit suicide, he would call me first. After his release from the hospital, Tam and I invited him to stay with us at our apartment. He stayed for a few weeks; the idea of returning to his parents' home was difficult and unsettling to him. By inviting Chris to stay with us, Tam and I were simply trying to help him recover from his illness of depression; unfortunately, we didn't realize that our lease stipulated that additional people were not allowed to stay with us, and we were evicted.

Eventually Chris moved on with his life and relocated to Philadelphia. There he got an apartment and found a wonderful partner who willingly accepted me as a friend. I often visited them while I was in college.

Eventually, I completed both my work-study and my student teaching. I did the latter at the shore resort of Rehoboth Beach, Delaware, where I taught third grade. It was a wonderful experience, as I loved both my cooperative teacher as well as my students, who were a lot of fun, eager to learn, and very respectful. Since I liked to cook, we did some cooking activities that nicely complemented our math lessons.

In December 1972, I finally achieved my alternate goal: completing school a semester early and finally making the dean's list, which was a major accomplishment. Yes, I had to settle for second best, since teaching was not my first love; however, I never lost my desire to work in the medical field. Spiritually speaking, I was still bordering on agnostic, but I was not as depressed as I had been. That first bout of deep depression lasted one year, and then life seemed to lighten up a bit.

In January 1973, I got my first teaching job at a middle school in New Castle, Delaware. I was confident and idealistic going into the classroom; after all, I'd had a very rewarding experience student teaching. At my new middle school job, things were quite different, for I was teaching seventh-grade math to classes whose size ranged from twenty-seven to thirty-three students. During the course of my job interview, I learned that the previous teacher (who had four children of her own and had taught math for fifteen years) had, one day in October, walked out of the classroom, never to return again! That should have been my first clue—a real red flag—that I was in for some interesting problems. The second clue—which also went right over my head—was that the students had had twenty-four substitutes between October and December! If I hadn't been so zealous about getting a teaching job, I might have heard what the principal was saying to me. Nevertheless, though fairly warned, I totally missed the point of my interviewer's words: I was walking into a war zone.

Once I arrived, my first order of business was to see where my students fell on the learning curve. To my amazement, there were some who didn't know their basic math facts, while others were ready for algebra and geometry. Unfortunately, all my classes were heterogeneous, a difficult situation to deal with and ultimately an absolute disaster. My initial instinct was to follow the guidelines of the philosophy I had learned in college, the concept of individualized teaching—which I immediately scrapped as being of no value in my present predicament, since I was trying to teach 163 students. Then I decided to cluster the kids into groups, but this task too was difficult to manage. Every day I had at least six lesson plans to develop, a job made all the harder because no math curriculum had even been *established* for the seventh grade, plus there were not enough textbooks of the same edition for any one group or class. (Even worse, the textbooks were from the 1940s, and this was 1973!) When I finally began writing out daily math sheets and running them off on the ditto machine every morning before school started, I was told I was using too much paper.

Being inexperienced and idealistic and dealing with kids from all walks of life and with different mathematical abilities and knowledge proved to be a ghastly struggle, and dealing with parental interference compounded the impossibilities. One parent, after requesting a parent-teacher conference concerning her chronically disruptive daughter, declared, "My daughter can talk to whoever she wants, whenever she wants, and can say whatever she wants." Trying to explain that this behavior was disruptive to the entire class and that other students were entitled to the best education I could give them was beyond this mother's comprehension. I was at a loss as to what to do. Detention was of no benefit to such students; it didn't change their behavior. Sending them to the principal's office was also futile, because it made it seem as though I was unable to control my classroom—which was true. Despite my early arrival at 7:00 a.m. and my daily departure at 5:00 p.m., I was unable to meet the daily demands of the job. Though I tried my best and worked hard to coordinate my methods of teaching math, I felt like a failure to a certain extent.

Upon arriving home in the evening, my roommate, Tam, and I would cook and eat dinner together and then isolate ourselves from 7:00 to 11:00 p.m., marking papers and preparing lessons, after which we would fall exhausted into bed. I was physically and emotionally drained from the stress of the job, but I also realized I'd been set up for failure by the school system. By the time my graduation exercises were formally held at the university in the spring of 1973, the stress of teaching for only six months had me down to a size-8 dress—the one thing out of the whole experience that made me happy.

In June 1973, I was told I had lost my job. I was disappointed but not totally upset. Ten other teachers had been let go too, although I was the first to lose my job, since I was the last hired. The reason we were given pink slips was that eleven hundred students were projected to leave the school district that year, including the more than four hundred students who would be graduating from high school. It was obvious that this district was qualitatively poor, and that parents who cared about their children's education and could afford to move were going to relocate to better school districts. This was no surprise to me.

What was surprising was that in July I received a call from the school district asking me to return to teach special education. Fortunately, I had decided to return to nursing school and was taking a summer science course, microbiology, so I had a legitimate excuse to decline the offer. I also told them I'd never had a course in special education the entire time I was in school. What went through my mind—but fortunately never came out of my mouth—was the question of how could they expect anyone to teach a special education class when they didn't have the supplies to teach a *regular* class.

That month I returned to the University of Delaware and entered the College of Nursing. I had finished all of my math courses and most of my science courses with the exception of microbiology, which I thoroughly enjoyed despite getting a C. (I did manage to get an A in microbiology lab.) Now I had only my nursing courses to take, most of which would net me six to twelve credits each. My attitude toward returning to school had changed; I still wanted to do well, but I had a more mature approach. I worked hard at my studies and worked equally hard on weekends, mostly at the neuroscience unit at the medical center, which proved fortuitous. My anxiety decreased because I felt somewhat less depressed and was doing well in my courses. My finances were better too. My grandfather died in December 1973 and left me five thousand dollars, enough to pay for the balance of my education, while what I earned at my job covered my living expenses. I also secured a job in the basic nursing lab. Life in general was better, and I was very thankful.

In the spring semester of 1974, I took a course in psychiatric nursing. My instructor was Miss S., a former nun and a very compassionate teacher. My practical experience was at the state hospital, where I worked with a schizophrenic patient I followed throughout the semester. She was a nice woman, and we spoke each week. Medication for schizophrenia was largely limited to Thorazine, which has the effect of turning patients into zombies. Despite our discussions of and planning for her discharge, my patient was unable to function once she went home. After a short stay there, she would have to return to the hospital, which made her sad. This was not my first experience with schizophrenia. I had a first cousin who suffered from it, and she too was frequently in and out of a mental hospital, but in Philadelphia. Whenever she was discharged, she constantly walked around the house appearing very flat, chain smoking and dusting furniture with a Kleenex. She didn't talk much, but when she did, she usually gave my aunt, who was a saint, a difficult time. In those days, psychiatric patients had to endure long and frequent hospitalizations, in part because effective treatments were not available. Little did I know that these experiences with mental illness would repeat themselves later in my life.

Miss S. realized that I had issues too. She perceived that my self-confidence was limited and that I had an inferiority complex. The latter was a product of my childhood, but I didn't know it then. Miss S. suggested that I see a therapist, and although I followed through with her recommendation, my health insurance allowed for only three visits. My therapist recommended Jerry Greenwald's book *Be the Person You Were Meant to Be,* and I tried to adopt its suggestions for gaining self-confidence and liking myself just the way I was. Although I found the book and the therapy helpful, getting to the root of my problems was impossible to do in three visits. At that time, I had no idea that this would be the beginning of many years of therapy, although I had already seen a psychiatrist once in high school.

I finished my course work for nursing in December 1975. Our only teacher for "little med-surg" (medical-surgical nursing) made everyone in her hospital rotation group neurotic, for she demanded excellence. She was right, of course; it's important to have a thorough knowledge of patients' problems before doing anything to or for them. She challenged us on each medication, expecting us to know all the side effects germane to it. Those of us under her tutelage tended to be uptight most of the time. Looking back, I can understand that her criticism was a justifiable part of training good nurses. But criticism had always been my Achilles' heel—another leftover from my childhood. In our next nursing course, which was maternal and child-health nursing, our instructors practically had to peel us off the ceiling because of our previous experience in little med-surg. In spite of our initial anxiety, we all landed on our feet and completed the rest of our course work without much anxiety. I graduated with honors and received a Sigma Theta Tau pin for excellence in nursing. Needless to say, I was proud of these personal accomplishments.

As usual, I wanted to work in a setting that I thought exemplified excellence. I therefore applied to the National Institute of Health in Bethesda, Maryland, where I was accepted and assigned to pediatric oncology. (I suspect I was put with children because I had a degree in elementary education.) It was there that I was taught much about oncology and chemotherapy. I also learned about research protocols and had the privilege of working with several pediatric oncologists. Pediatric oncology was a relatively new specialty at the time, and many of those doctors went on to head up pediatric oncology programs in major teaching hospitals, such as Children's Hospital in Boston.

People used to ask me, "How can you work with children who have cancer? Isn't that depressing?" My reply would be that although many of the children died—there were children from all over the world who had met the criteria of the research studies the NCI was conducting—early on I adopted the attitude that my responsibility was not to cure them, but to take care of them and provide comfort to them and their parents. Actually I became very close to some of the families, despite their pain of suffering the loss of a child. As they struggled with potentially terminal diseases, I tried to bring a little joy into their lives while providing the best nursing care I knew how to give. Most of the nursing staff supported one another, and so working with dying children was not difficult for us. None of us actually became depressed or left the pediatric oncology units because of depression. It was at this time too that I met my husband-to-be, and his love helped ease any depression left over from my college years.

Eventually I asked to work on the bone marrow transplant unit, known as the Laminar Flow Unit. There we initiated autologous bone marrow transplants, which are like the stem cell transplants of today. Eventually I was asked to be a preceptor and speak at conferences, which helped improve my self-confidence and reduce my tendency to retreat into my sad moods and isolate myself. I still had doubts about God, but that was also changing little by little. What was obviously changing was my self-confidence; I was becoming more self-assured because I was regarded as an excellent nurse. It wasn't obvious to me at the time, but my self-appraisal was actually a function of what others thought of me. All this would be significant in my future life, though I did not see it at that time.

The allegorical poem "Footprints in the Sand" is reminiscent of my life. I was not always aware that God was holding me up in many ways. Interestingly, although this lovely and inspirational poem is often credited to various authors, the official author is Mary Stevenson. I have been given permission to use this poem, but only in e-books. Thus, in order to have the book printed, I needed to modify a portion of it.

Footprints in the Sand

One night a man had a dream. He dreamed he was walking along the beach with the Lord. Across the sky flashed scenes from his life. For each scene he noticed two sets of footprints in the sand: *The poem continues with the man noticing that at times there was only one set of footprints in the sand, and these were times when the man was most conflicted. He says the following to the Lord:* "I don't understand why, when I need you the most, You would leave me." The Lord replied, "My son, my precious child, I love you and I would *never* leave you. During your time of trial and suffering, when you see only one set of footprints, it was then that I *carried* you."

Chapter 6

Our Early Married Life

It was a lovely warm evening in May 1977 when I met my husband-to-be. My cousin Har and his wonderful wife, Ann, had invited me up from Maryland to have dinner with one of Har's longtime friends, Arthur Taylor. Har and Arthur had played Tiny Tot Basketball together as children at the Northeast Boys Club in Frankford, later becoming part of the staff and good friends. For a long time Har had been saying to Arthur, "You should meet my cousin. You would really like her." And so, on that warm May evening, Har and Ann made it possible for Arthur and me to meet. Ann cooked an outstanding dinner, after which we sat around the table and chatted for hours. First impressions are often lasting ones; despite being extremely overweight, Arthur was a nice, friendly guy who was also quite intelligent, ambitious, warmhearted, religious, and family oriented. Just before leaving for our respective homes at the end of the evening, Arthur said to me, "You should come down to the boat some weekend." So we exchanged telephone numbers and parted—Arthur for the home he shared with his parents, and me for my mother's Philadelphia home, where I stayed during my frequent visits from Bethesda. I was surprised to discover that our homes were less than two miles apart.

The story could have ended there, but I decided to make the initial call rather than waiting for Arthur to act. I called him from work one night during a break, asking if I might come up to Cape May for a weekend visit with him and his family. Unfortunately, the weekend I suggested for my visit was Memorial Day weekend, and Arthur apologetically explained that his aunt, uncle, and two cousins had already made plans to visit, thus allowing no room on the boat for anyone else. Being a nurse, I had few free weekends; however, I did have days off during the week, and so I suggested that we meet in Philadelphia during one of my trips from Bethesda to visit my mother. This instigated nightly telephone conversations, and when I was scheduled to be off work on June 14 and 15, a Tuesday and Wednesday, Arthur invited me to dinner. I immediately accepted. He took me to an old stone house called the Golden Pheasant, which had a greenhouse attached to the building. Inside the greenhouse there was a patio garden containing ficus trees festooned with tiny white lights and candles glowing in antique cast-iron holders. Not only was the setting perfect for intimate conversation, but the service was wonderful, the food delicious, and the company awesome. It was a perfect romantic night, during which we lingered over wine and chateaubriand for several hours. When the check came—it was more than eighty dollars—Arthur picked up the tab. That was a lot of money in 1977! I kept thinking, *Wow! This is the best date I've ever been on in my life*! Arthur treated me like a princess—something I'd never before experienced—and I was smitten.

Upon leaving the Golden Pheasant, both of us were totally relaxed but tired. He had worked that day, and I had driven up from Bethesda the previous night after working the evening shift. While driving me to my mother's house, Arthur nearly nodded off many times. I watched him carefully, continuing our conversation in an effort to keep him awake. Although I felt anxious about the entire return trip, we arrived safely at my mother's home, where we kissed good night—a wonderfully romantic first kiss. I knew on that first date that I was going to marry him, for it was true love at first sight for both of us.

We were engaged in August 1977 and married on December 10 of the same year. Arthur was thirty, and I was two weeks away from twenty-seven. We wasted no time in getting married, because we both agreed that at our age we knew what we were looking for in a partner. After all, back in those days, most young people married either directly after high school or immediately after acquiring a college degree. We were obviously the exception.

Prior to the wedding, we rented a lovely, large condo in Maple Shade, New Jersey, where I lived from October to December because it was closer to work. I brought all my furniture except my twin beds. Arthur and I went looking for furniture for our bedroom, and he decided he wanted colonial furniture from Ethan Allen's. Although that was not my style, I was not about to debate the issue; some things are just not worth arguing about. After Arthur picked out what he wanted, the salesperson said to him, "Do you want a mattress and box spring to go with that?"—to which Arthur, in all seriousness, replied, "You mean to tell me they don't come with the furniture?" He had obviously not learned about how expensive things were, having lived at home all his life and paying his parents only twenty-five dollars a week once he started working after college.

The other life lesson Arthur was unprepared for occurred during our first grocery shopping trip. Used to being well fed, he methodically added more and more items to our shopping cart, so that it was full by the time we reached the checkout counter. The total bill came to $54— equivalent to $219 in 2016, accounting for inflation. Arthur could not believe we had spent that much; he was totally flabbergasted at the cost of food. Neither shopping experience surprised me, for I had been living on my own since I was eighteen years old and had already been initiated into the mysterious world of finances.

The spirit and joy of preparing for our wedding were temporarily dampened by two events. The first occurred at the rehearsal dinner, when Arthur's mother said to him in my presence, "I wish you were marrying Carol." This made me feel terrible, and I started to lose respect for my soon-to-be mother-in-law. (Although I always was gracious to her and thankful for all the kind things she did for our family, I was slow to forgive. She was a kind person but an alcoholic. It was when she was imbibing, which was nearly every day, that she was nasty to me.) Her comment was not just unnecessary; it was also insulting to Arthur and me on the eve of our wedding.

The second event was that Arthur's father couldn't attend the wedding, as he'd been hospitalized with complications from a botched aortic aneurysm resection. On the day of the ceremony, Arthur called and suggested we have a hospital bedside wedding ceremony first so that his father could see us get married, after which we would go to the church where the official ceremony would be held. Quite innocently I shared this idea with my mother, and she flipped out. As I still couldn't say no to anyone, I was stuck between my husband-to-be and my own mother. Fortunately, Arthur agreed to visit his father in the hospital between the end of the Mass and the beginning of the reception—a suggestion that only a man of his temperament would have adopted, keeping the peace at the expense of his own wishes.

A far less upsetting event—and one that we could laugh about in later years—was that the chauffeur who picked up the bridesmaids and flower girl somehow forgot the bride! Not until the organist was about to play the wedding march did Arthur realize I wasn't there. In a sudden scramble, he arranged to have me picked up while the organist played additional music.

Nevertheless, we had a wonderful wedding. I made my wedding gown with the help of my mother and my aunt and her sister, who sewed on the lace appliqués. We wrote our own vows and had "Love Is Eternal" inscribed in our gold wedding bands (the title of a historical fiction book about Mary Todd Lincoln written by Irving Stone in

1954). The lovely marriage ceremony was conducted by Arthur's good friend Father John. Instead of following the traditional custom of the groom and his men forming a line at the front of the church to await the bride's arrival at the altar, we adopted a Jewish practice I had seen in a bridal magazine, in which both the bride and the groom walk down the aisle with their parents (although in this case, of necessity, we were accompanied only by our mothers). I thought this procession was more family oriented, and Arthur readily agreed. During the ceremony I had to prompt Arthur with the recitation of the vows, but that was all right—I was truly in love.

With all the excitement and the added responsibilities, I was ravenously hungry after the reception. When I told Arthur, he exclaimed, "You mean to tell me that you're starving after the most expensive dinner of your *life?*" After changing into our "going away outfits" and gathering up our luggage, we went to the Penrose Avenue Diner (a well-known eatery in Philadelphia), where we shared a corned beef sandwich at 3:00 a.m. Then we drove to the hotel near the Philadelphia airport, where I was appropriately carried over the threshold of our hotel room—and the rest is history.

The next morning we left for our honeymoon at one of Arthur's favorite spots, a Rock Resort in Virgin Gorda, one of the British Virgin Islands. He had chosen a magnificent, wonderfully warm place, which was just what we needed, considering we left Philadelphia on one of the coldest, iciest, windiest days in December. We flew into Puerto Rico, where we transferred onto a very small prop plane that would take us to the island. The size of the plane necessitated careful balancing of the weight of the passengers and luggage, which made Arthur a ringer due to his large size. Once all was balanced, we took off successfully. Looking down as our tiny plane approached the island, I saw a dirt path carved into the mountainside. This, Arthur explained, was to be our landing strip, to which I muttered a skeptical, "Right!" But we landed safely.

The resort was beautiful, with individual breezy, spacious rooms with ceiling fans and slatted blinds on the windows. The twin beds were European in style, similar to those sold by Ikea, with wooden slats for a box spring and then a mattress over it with beautiful linens. Unfortunately, the slats tended to fall apart every time we turned over. Our request for wooden boards over the bed slats was immediately granted. I am sure we were not the first or last guests to be unceremoniously dumped out of bed and onto the floor, which definitely wasn't conducive to making love! Still, it was an amazing resort with delicious food, beautiful white beaches, and crystal-clear blue water with multicolored fish just beneath the surface. We snorkeled in the Baths, rock formations near the resort which are similar to those at Stonehenge in England.

The trip was a dream come true—until I got food poisoning from drinking tainted pineapple juice on a side trip to Tortola. When we arrived on the island at 11:00 a.m. after a bumpy ride on a watercraft known as the Bombba Charger, Arthur suggested we get something to drink. I ordered pineapple juice while he ordered a piña colada. The bartender used the remains of an already-open can of pineapple juice for me, then opened a new can for Arthur's drink. I felt sick on the way back from Tortola, as we raced from island to island. Either I was seasick, or something else was brewing. All I knew was that I was feeling distinctly green! Once we were on terra firma, I was *still* feeling green, and subsequently I got very, very ill. I was unable to stop vomiting and suffered from severe stomach cramps. Arthur, alarmed and fearful that I would die on our honeymoon, tried to contact a doctor but found there was none on the island of Virgin Gorda. However, he was able to reach a physician who resided on another island, and was assured that I was in no danger of dying. The doctor's predictions were correct, and within days I was feeling well enough to take a pleasant boat ride to a desolate island where the two of us relaxed for several hours while enjoying gourmet boxed lunches. With the exception of the tainted pineapple juice, our honeymoon turned out to be perfect.

We arrived home one week before Christmas, just in time to do some shopping for our families. Since my birthday fell on December 24, Arthur and I were invited to my sister's home for Christmas Eve. Arthur insisted we attend midnight Mass—the first one I ever attended. It was held at my sister's parish church, and by the time we arrived, there was standing room only. Having had an extremely busy month, Arthur literally fell asleep standing up at the back of the church, thus affording me the first experience of seeing someone sleep on his feet. After Mass we immediately went home and fell into bed.

Because this was our first Christmas as a married couple, both our families wanted us to come to their homes for Christmas dinner, which was impossible, of course, and placed us in a quandary that I hoped would correct itself. We actually shared time with both families, eating two large meals and thus being very full and tired at the end of the day. It was the first and last time this happened; for future holiday meals, I cooked and our families joined us in our home.

Arthur's father (also named Arthur) was still in the hospital, suffering from several complications resulting from an aortic aneurysm resection. He had been scheduled for surgery in October with the full expectation of being well enough to participate in our wedding in December. Unfortunately, when it came time to resect the aneurysm, the surgeons clamped off the renal arteries for too long, throwing him into renal failure, which ultimately required him to have dialysis. Additionally, some plaque formations sloughed off his arteries and descended into his lower limbs, necessitating partial amputation of one leg. It was February 1978 before he got out of the hospital, and June before he was independent. Arthur's mother was legally blind and unable to drive, so she would take public transportation to the hospital every day to see her sick husband. After work each night, my newlywed husband would visit his father and then chauffeur his mother back to her home in Philadelphia before driving back to our rented condo in Maple Shade. Being a faithful son, he also took over the management of his father's painting company in Philadelphia. Despite all this responsibility, he never complained. I must confess that I was somewhat bent out of shape—this was not what I had anticipated as a start to our marriage—but I didn't complain either. I knew this was the way things had to be, considering that Arthur was an only child and there was no one else to lighten his parents' burden.

While Arthur worked as a painting estimator for his father's business in Philadelphia, I worked at a hospital in Burlington County, New Jersey, as its first oncology nurse. My hours were long, because I often had to administer chemotherapy late in the afternoon, after the orders were written. I worked with two, and then three, outstanding medical oncologists. Dr. Flinker, who was up-to-date on data regarding treatment protocols for cancer patients, was the driving force behind the practice. He had joined the Eastern Cooperative Oncology Group, and we initially collaborated with Jefferson Hospital. Meanwhile, I managed the collection and recording of data on patients who participated in the research protocols. As the practice expanded, Dr. Samuels from the University of Pennsylvania joined our staff, followed by Dr. Michael Krachermacher, a Duke University graduate who was recruited from a hospital in the Worcester, Massachusetts, area. Other physicians were brought into the practice as it expanded. It was an honor to work in such a well-staffed community hospital where there were so many talented physicians and such compassionate and intelligent nurses.

Somehow, in the midst of my husband's responsibilities concerning his parents and his job, and my own job at the hospital, I managed to get pregnant in March 1978. Ideas about the best time to get pregnant have radically changed over the past forty years. People now wait until their late thirties or early forties before starting a family. But in the 1970s, the emphasis was on having children before age thirty. Fortunately, my pregnancy was uneventful, with the exception of my being very tired during the first three months. During that period I would come home from work, flop onto the couch, and fall asleep. We needed to eat out because I was too tired to cook; consequently, I gained a lot of weight and so did Arthur. We joked a lot about both of us being pregnant— except I eventually lost the weight, and he didn't!

The fall of 1978 was an incredibly busy time for us. During our first year of marriage, we saved my paycheck toward a down payment for a house. I had always wanted to live near the hospital, which would cut down on my driving between work and home. I needed as much time at home as I could get, as the majority of household responsibilities were mine, plus I would be caring for however many children we might have. So we bought a 128-year-old house near the hospital, making numerous necessary renovations prior to moving there in October 1978. Some of them were invisible, such as replacing the knob-and-tube wiring. A more visible renovation was sanding and varnishing the wide-plank floors. We also purchased drapes for the windows, put down a new kitchen floor, redid the powder room, and put a large closet in the master bedroom, since closet space was traditionally scare in homes that old.

In the fall of 1978, we also started taking childbirth classes. I wanted to have our children naturally. Arthur faithfully attended the classes with me and became a great coach. Since I had an affinity for frogs, he bought me a large, green stuffed frog to use as my focal point during labor. About 8:30 on the evening of our last class, we were walking down the street to our car when my water broke and the contractions started. Since Arthur had to square things away with his numerous jobs before he could take me to the hospital, I gathered my personal items and then waited until 1:00 a.m. before we could be on our way! This wasn't something I had anticipated; I still had a lot to learn about being the wife of a business owner. By the time we met my doctor at the hospital, which was about twenty miles away, I was seven centimeters effaced and three centimeters dilated. (The sixty-four bags of leaves I had raked, bagged, and hauled to the curb the previous day *might* have had something to do with that.) Luckily, the delivery was uncomplicated, and our first child, Edward, was born at 3:15 a.m.—a a joyous occasion for both my husband and me.

I continued to work at the local hospital until June 1989. In the interim, between Edward's birth in 1978 and the birth of our second child, James, in April 1981, we impulsively sold our home near the hospital and moved to a brand-new house in Tabernacle, New Jersey. This was farther away from work for both Arthur and me, but in 1980, Tabernacle was a lovely area. We stayed there about four years. It was there that James was born and Edward attended kindergarten.

James was born four days after Easter. Two days after his due date, the contractions began, so we headed for the hospital in Marlton, New Jersey. By the time we arrived, my contractions were very close together, and I was immediately rushed to the delivery room. The fact that this was my second delivery facilitated the speed at which the baby was born, so my labor lasted only about three hours. Arthur and the doctor were conversing outside the delivery room when the labor and delivery nurse approached them with the admonishment, "If you want to be present for this delivery, you better get into the delivery room right now!" And just about the same time, out popped our second child.

Arthur's father died of congestive heart failure not long afterward. This left Arthur's mother alone, but fortunately she and my mother were the best of friends. They often went down to the shore together.

I stayed home with James for three months, as I had with Edward, and then my neighbor took care of both boys while I went back to work. But when they both contracted the chicken pox in the summer of 1982, my neighbor decided to stop taking care of them. James's case was rather mild, but Edward had serious issues with the disease, developing periorbital cellulitis (swelling of the tissues around the eye), which had him in and out of hospitals throughout the summer. This was the impetus for me to quit working full-time, which was in one respect disappointing, as I had been made head nurse of the hospital's first oncology unit, which I had personally organized with help from Dr. Flinker, administered, and staffed with registered nurses. I also developed and helped teach a two-week course in chemotherapy and general oncology. Nevertheless, I knew my family had to come first.

After Edward and James had the chicken pox, my husband developed a serious case of cellulitis in his leg (one of many such cases he would have in his lifetime). He was over it around Labor Day. We had not been down to the shore house since the Fourth of July due to one illness after another. While we were there for Labor Day weekend, I noticed Arthur's mother was acting a bit strange. I could not put my finger on what was happening, but she seemed to have some cognitive confusion. I told Arthur to take his mother to the nearby hospital, which he did, but they could not find anything wrong with her and sent her home. Two days later she had a severe stroke that affected her left side for which she was hospitalized. After her discharge from the hospital, she stayed with us until November. Then in November she had a carotid endarterectomy to reduce the possibility of further strokes. It was difficult taking care of her, because she was diabetic and liked to drink Scotch by the half gallon. Additionally, she was on Decadron, a steroid, which made her very hungry. This combination of habits, medications, and underlying illness was a challenge for me to manage, not to mention the additional challenge of having two little boys at home. Being a nurse, I was very meticulous about her diabetic diet. She lost a fair amount of weight and recovered most of the use of her left side except for some foot drop. I was exhausted after she left for her own home. It had been a long summer and autumn.

I decided to go back to work on weekends on the oncology unit, where I could answer any questions the other nurses had, as I had the most experience with oncology patients. This change turned out to be distressing for me in two ways. First, the new head nurse felt threatened when I assisted the other nurses. Second, Arthur was not very good at getting the kids dressed; I would come home from work and find them wearing their clothes from the night before. I was both disappointed and angry that Arthur was not taking better care of them.

Shortly after that, we moved to a very nice and friendly town in Burlington County, New Jersey, which was closer to Arthur's new office. Arthur's father's business had been located in a rather unsavory part of Philadelphia, and in 1980, after multiple break-ins at Arthur's business office (which suffered three robberies in one week), Arthur decided to relocate the office to Pennsauken, New Jersey. The new property consisted of a reception room, a spacious office, and a large amount of storage space for painting equipment. The building offered two additional plusses: it was closer to where we lived, and it was in a much safer location. These were important attributes for everyone concerned.

A couple of years after our move to our affluent community in New Jersey, my mother decided to move in with us to help with the kids. Prior to our marriage, Arthur and I had discussed the matter of adopting a child—an idea that I had started researching before meeting my husband, for I knew that even if I never married, I wanted to have a child. There were so many children in the world in need of love and parenting that I felt it was unnecessary for me to ever give birth to one myself. Many families in our community and the surrounding areas had adopted Korean children, so with that thought in mind, Arthur and I applied to adopt a child through Holt International Children's Services, an organization with offices in New Jersey and several other states. After completing the entire screening and interview process, we were selected to be adoptive parents. Since we already had two biological boys, we were permitted to ask for a girl. We made the request even more challenging because we didn't want a newborn. I had taken care of newborn babies twice before, and I didn't need that experience again! We were told that our request could possibly delay the process, because older children were harder to find and place. Nevertheless, shortly afterward, in December 1985, we received a picture of an adorable girl named Song, Song

Ee, standing on a chair wearing a white fleece suit. Along with the photo, we received the information that her mother was unmarried and worked in the kitchen of a restaurant. During the 1970s and '80s, unwed mothers in Korea were shunned by their families. We learned that this child had been carried on her mother's back until she was almost two, at which point the mother gave her up, which had to have been heartbreaking for the poor woman. Judging from the photo, Song Ee was a petite girl, and additional information indicated she liked to sing and dance. Also, we were told her birthday was in December, which convinced us that she was right for our family, as so many important events happened that month—Edward's birthday, our wedding anniversary, my birthday, and Christmas. We received Song Ee on March 7, 1986, just two days before Arthur's birthday. Little did I know she would be glued to my hip for the rest of my life. She also would become one of my guardian angels.

Once again I stayed home for three months to take care of the children. My mother had become difficult at times, having grown increasingly critical of the two boys, my husband, and me, and now she began to say some rather cruel things about our new daughter. As it often happens, however, she learned to adore and appreciate our adopted daughter, whose Korean name, Song, we kept. Admittedly, the children were a handful, but the real problem for Mom was that at age seventy, she was too old to be around little children continuously. So it was necessary to implement another childcare plan. Edward was in first grade and doing well. James, meanwhile, went to Montessori school and was doing amazingly well; he knew the names of all the oceans and continents at three years of age. But Mom found it very stressful to pick him up each day. The one problem with James was that he didn't pay attention. He was very intelligent but was often off in his own world. By the time he had reached the age of four, my education in teaching and nursing led me to suspect that he had some learning and behavioral issues. These persistent red flags of not paying attention, not following directions, and doing what he wanted to do all the time followed him through kindergarten and into first grade. Finally, in second grade, I had him evaluated, and he was diagnosed as having attention deficit disorder.

Meanwhile, Mom was having difficulty even helping me with our new daughter, despite the fact that Song had learned English within three months of being in the United States and was a pleasant child who was easy to care for. So I hired a lady from our church, Christine, who had two adopted Korean children of her own. Chris did a wonderful job with the children while I was at work, and she took care of my house as well. But we soon learned that Song also had learning issues, so we decided to send her to two kindergartens—St. Charles School in Cinnaminson in the morning, and the local public school in our community each afternoon. At noon each school day, Chris would pick up Song at St. Charles School, give her lunch at home, change her out of her uniform and into regular clothes, and then take her to the public school. I will always be grateful for all her attention to our children and our home. She provided the best childcare situation we ever had. Even my mother liked Chris, which was a plus!

After James was born, Arthur and I agreed that I should have my tubes tied, for it seemed likely that as easily as I got pregnant, we'd end up with a baseball team if we didn't do something about birth control. I was told that the procedure could be reversed but there was no guarantee I could get pregnant again. However, at the age of forty-two, with my biological clock slowing down, I told Arthur I would like to have another child. His exact words were, "Shoot me first!" His message was quite clear, and so the adoption of Song ended the expansion of our family. In the long run, I'm glad Arthur had the insight not to agree to any more children.

Meanwhile, Arthur's business continued to do well for several years, after which Arthur closed his company and worked for two of his competitors in Philadelphia. In February 1995, while he was home with another serious bout of cellulitis, he realized that the company he was working for was going under. He immediately began pursuing a job as a painting estimator, ultimately joining a large painting company in Massachusetts in June 1995. I remained in New Jersey for another year, trying to sell the house and manage the family, which was rapidly getting out of control, creating a real challenge for me since I was working full-time.

Chapter 7

Rearing Children:
A Difficult Job

$\mathcal{R}$earing children is not easy for anyone. Our pediatrician, Dr. T., recommended that we have our children three years apart. Perhaps we should have listened to him regarding the birth of our boys. If we had followed his advice, it might have made a difference, but my husband and I did what we thought was best at the time.

Rearing our children was particularly complicated because all five of us tended to suffer from ill health. Frequent bouts of illness are stressful for any family, and most of our family's illnesses were chronic and unremitting. Arthur's were physical; Edward's were both physical and psychological; James's were totally psychological; Song's were learning disabilities; and mine were due to mental illness. Often only one person in the family was ill, but at other times several of us were sick at once, and that made family life very difficult. Arthur was the only one suffering from a terminal illness, a genetic one that we did not know about until close to the end of his life. Perhaps the rest of the family's illnesses were genetic too, with the exception of our daughter's, whose medical history we never received when we adopted her. As life went on and my mother's family grew older, it became apparent that mental illness ran in her family; several of my cousins and my one aunt had it. I believe my mother was depressed too, but I would say it was a situational depression from the trauma in her married life, which remained undiagnosed until she was ninety years old. Once it was diagnosed and treated, she was a different, happier person.

However, there were many mutually enjoyable times despite our physical and mental illnesses. Arthur, the eternal optimist, was always happy and living in the moment—always generous and supportive toward each of us, regardless of the financial cost. He was, however, quite stubborn; he rarely changed his mind, despite what I defined as his impractical thinking. He often lived in denial, sticking his head in the sand even if the situation touched him or someone else in the family. Though he liked being taken care of, it was always on his terms.

Unlike Arthur, I was very practical. I considered myself a realist (though some would say I was a pessimist). Unfortunately, I was always striving to accommodate other people's needs. I loved to make people feel happy and welcome, always trying to do my best. True, I would advocate for myself, but my entreaties for my own needs usually fell on deaf ears. This and my prior life events led to my being depressed much of my married life (from 1989 on), but I always tried to work through the tough times despite the depression. Though I worked professionally as a nurse, I unfortunately earned less money than Arthur most of our married life. Despite being a devoted wife, mother, and daughter and trying to pull in the reins financially, I was unsuccessful in the financial realm; I was living with a Pisces who was very generous and liked to spend money we didn't really have. And I was stubborn too, which turned out not to work in my favor either. Arthur saw me as the mommy, the teacher, the nurse, the caretaker, and the doer of all things except those having to do with finances. My only responsibility in *that* department was to make sure the medical bills were paid and any issues were resolved. Arthur had no interest in making sure our medical expenses were covered; he seemed to feel that whatever insurance covered was all the medical community deserved. I was a Capricorn, a goat whose feet were always planted on solid ground. But despite the kind of differences and problems most married couples have, Arthur and I loved each other.

Our oldest son, Edward, seemed happy as an infant, but as he grew older he became more aloof. As a toddler, his two favorite words were *keys* and *Mc-Don-olds*. The severe case of chicken pox that he had when he was three resulted in periorbital cellulitis and inappropriate ADH syndrome. (The chicken pox vaccine was not readily available to healthy children at that time.) IADHS is a buildup of fluids in the body and a subsequent lowering of sodium in the system. This can lead to a decrease of fluids in the brain. Although the treatment sounds counterintuitive, restricting fluids, and sometimes adding sodium, is recommended. Edward was sick from the Fourth of July until the third week in August 1982.

When Edward was four, we took him to Disney World, which he loved. He had breakfast with some of the cartoon characters, but after he finished eating, he crawled under the dining table and fell asleep! Unfortunately, Edward never seemed to get along with his brother, James, although he was able to make friends with other children in his childcare facility and at school. When his sister joined our family, he got along with her—so it seemed to be only James whom he disliked. But despite our encouraging him to try and get along with his brother, Edward had his own ideas and wouldn't change. All in all, however, he was a cute kid, and he quickly became the apple of his paternal grandmother's eye.

As Edward matured, he became ambitious, working hard on things in which he had an interest, especially if money was involved. If there was a fundraiser, he would be the first one on the job, collecting the most money or selling the most items. On the other hand, he was a complete slob; his bedroom was a total disaster when he was a teenager.

I always told him what goes around comes around, and now he has a teenage son who is unbelievably messy—while Edward is now extremely organized. Who would have thought?

In school, Edward's work was fair but not great—he simply wasn't interested. Actually he was very smart, but not when it came to academics. Eventually he dropped out of high school, went to an alternative school for a short period of time, dropped out of *that,* and then got his GED without studying. He also developed into a go-getter and was artistically talented. He loved to play ice hockey as a teenager, but because his own high school had no hockey team, he played four years for Holy Cross, the Catholic high school in a nearby community. He was also a part of the Bristol Blazers, a club team in Bristol, Pennsylvania. I remember one Holy Cross game when he played almost the entire game because there had been a snowstorm and many of his teammates failed to show up. He would rest atop the boards because he didn't have the energy to go over them to sit on the bench, since he was out on the ice for almost the entire game.

Edward could be thoughtful, but always on his own terms. Once when he was at Pat's Steaks (a famous steak sandwich place in Philadelphia), eating a large cheese steak lathered with Cheez Whiz, a homeless man approached him asking for money. Not having any, Edward gave the homeless man half his sandwich. That's how good-hearted he could be. As a teenager, he and Bradford (one of his best friends even to this day) built a very nice tree house in Brad's backyard. Unfortunately they didn't have a building permit, and one of the neighbors insisted it be removed. So down it came without incident. He and Bradford also had a small lawn mowing business at which they worked very hard. Arthur and I were glad Edward and Bradford were friends, for we felt that Bradford was a good example for our son.

At age thirteen, Edward entered a rebellious stage that continued through his teenage years. Because he was difficult to manage, we signed up for family counseling at Children's Hospital in Philadelphia, but Edward flatly refused to go. Realizing the necessity of Edward's presence at the session, his father promised him a new pair of hockey skates (no cheap investment) if he would go to the psychologist with the rest of the family. With this deal in hand, Edward agreed, but he never uttered a word during any of the sessions. Since he went, however, Arthur made good on the deal. Consequently we had eight weeks of videotaped sessions of the family's interactions, including lots of complaints about Edward from everyone else in the family, including James—who was no saint either. Then after all *that,* the psychologist diagnosed Edward as having an unspecified personality disorder. This means that Edward did not meet the criteria of any of the subcategories of a personality disorder—which makes sense, since Edward never said a word and the psychologist could only determine a diagnosis based on the information that the rest of the family shared during the eight sessions.

What was frustrating for me was that we did not have a clue or recommendation about how to manage Edward, so he went on doing as he pleased without regard for our wishes. (More accurately, Edward rarely listened to me but would pay attention to his father, because he wanted to skate and his father wanted him to skate too.) I felt totally ignored, which was infuriating because I was the one trying to teach him manners, such as the need to tell us where he was going and when he would be back.

When Edward was fourteen, he secretly took my car out of the garage while I was sitting in the family room waiting for Arthur to come home from a business meeting. When Arthur arrived home, he immediately asked me, "Where's your car?" to which I responded, "It's in the garage." He assured me that my car was not in the garage, which prompted me to rush upstairs and look for Edward—who of course wasn't there. Furthermore, his window was open and the shingles on the roof overhanging the front entryway into the house were in disarray. We soon discovered that Edward had picked up one of his hoodlum friends, of which he had many (with the exception of Brad), and they had decided to drive down to Florida to go deep-sea fishing! The two of them got as far as North Carolina before they determined that they didn't have enough money to complete the trip or to fish. Meanwhile, we tried to have Edward listed as a missing child, but we discovered that he had to be missing for forty-eight hours before the police would even consider him missing. (In those days, there was no such thing as an Amber Alert.) At the same time, the boys had turned around and started driving back toward home—but when they reached the Maryland-Delaware border, they had no money to pay the toll on Interstate 95. (There was no such thing as E-ZPass either; otherwise, I'm sure they would have tried to run the toll lane.) As it turned out, at 11:00 p.m. we received a phone call from Edward asking if *we* could come down and meet them to pay the toll. Though we were hugely relieved to know where he was, Arthur and I were angry about what he had done. It took us more than an hour to drive down from our home to reach Edward and his friend, after which we separated the boys—I drove Edward's friend home in silence in my car, and Arthur headed home with Edward in his. Only God, my husband, and Edward know what was said en route, but whatever it was, the car was never "borrowed" again.

At the age of fourteen, Edward got his first job at McDonald's. Obviously he knew how to drive, and so at sixteen (with driver's license in hand) he purchased a very old, very large, blue Buick Electra with the money he'd saved from his McDonald's paychecks. (Arthur and I had purchased his first car for him, but it didn't run very long. As the mechanic observed: "What do you expect for four hundred and fifty dollars?") Arthur referred to Edward's enormous Buick as a "cop magnet," and it was.

At sixteen, with my husband now living in Massachusetts and the rest of us still in New Jersey, Edward did whatever he pleased, completely ignoring anything I said. He would take off with his friends without telling me where he was going or when he would be home.

In addition, he would tell me to f--- off in reply to anything I asked him to do. In other words, he was becoming increasingly difficult to manage. I even went to the Division of Youth and Family Services for help; I had reached my limit and didn't know what to do with him. The courts ordered him to be placed in foster housing for three weeks, after which he returned home a little less contrary. However, the story does not end there.

At age seventeen, he got his girlfriend pregnant. Although Arthur and I suggested they give the child up for adoption, the girl's father said, "No blood child of mine is going to be given up for adoption." This conviction was admirable in theory, but the girl's parents never contributed a dime toward the care of the baby, who was named Nathan. At four months of age, Nathan became the *fifth* child in our house, for in addition to Edward, James, and Song, we also took in little Nathan's mother. To Edward's credit, he always worked to support his child, and now he has full custody of Nathan after many years of wrangling with the court system in Massachusetts, which is very pro-mother.

When the baby was born, my mother said, "Christine, Nathan is going to become very important in your life," a prophecy that came true. But our relationship still has not developed into a very comfortable one. Though we enjoy moments of being the best of buddies, and although he sometimes refers to me as Mom, Nathan is following in the footsteps of his father in terms of his rebelliousness and disrespectful behavior. Though I love Nathan, who is now nineteen, I don't like most of his behavior and his general attitude toward me, himself, and other people. I hope that within the next few years, his thinking will mature and we can become close again.

Meanwhile, Edward has become a good father to all three of his children. In addition to Nathan, he now has two girls—one is two years old and the other is five—by a different girlfriend. He has developed into a responsible person, an outcome I doubted for several years. He has helped me out when I really needed him, a gesture for which I will always feel grateful, and now he even *listens* to me, sometimes. Most of the time I know where I stand with him; he tells me exactly what he is thinking. At times I feel like I'm walking on eggshells with him, which I find uncomfortable, for I have to be very careful with what I say to him. I know he loves me, but he is not at all affectionate—perhaps because he is a Sagittarius.

Since Arthur and I had decided before James was born that he would be our last biological child, I had my tubes tied while I was still in the hospital. James was a relatively small baby, six pounds and seven ounces, but he seemed healthy and took to nursing right away. After trying to nurse him for three months, however, I was convinced that nursing was futile. It was clear to me that he did not like my milk. We eventually put him on Isomil. He also was not fond of vegetables, which seemed to give him colic.

One day while James was still in his bassinet, his older brother presented him to us while carrying him by the head! To say the least, I was shocked. In retrospect, this was probably the most endearing act of kindness Edward ever displayed toward his brother.

As an infant, James was fussy and needed a lot of physical soothing; usually rubbing his arm quieted him down. The same neighbor cared for James and Edward until both boys caught the chicken pox. At that point I had to quit my job as the head nurse of the newly developed oncology unit, which was disappointing to me, but I knew I needed to do it.

In 1984, our family moved to a new town that was closer to George's work. James was three and went to the local Montessori School. He seemed to like the format there, as he was able to explore things that interested him. He loved geography, and by the time he was three he knew all the continents and oceans and where they were. His main problem was a lack of concentration and cooperation. He was not a bad child, just a challenge. By the time he was four, I knew he had some issues. Although I pointed out the red flags to Arthur—lack of focus, difficulty concentrating, uncooperativeness, failure to follow directions—he did not buy into any of my insights. By the time James was in second grade, he was diagnosed with ADD. Dr. Williams did some behavior modification with James, and he worked with me so I would have the tools to help James with his schoolwork. Despite all our efforts, James seemed to need more help and was started on Ritalin. His pediatrician, Dr. Carlos, kept increasing his doses because the lower ones were ineffective.

I remember once, when James was ten, having to wait more than two hours to see Dr. Carlos, who wanted to change James's medication from Ritalin to Dexedrine. Although I appreciated the fact that Dr. Carlos provided thorough care for each patient, trying to keep a child with ADD occupied for two hours while waiting for a scheduled appointment was insanity. James was losing it and so was I. I thought about leaving the office, but it would have been difficult to get a follow-up visit. It truly was a no-win situation.

Before James went on this new stimulant, Dr. Carlos wanted him to have an EKG and blood work. Unfortunately, his office did not do these procedures. I was eager to get James started on the new medication, as his behavior was becoming more and more difficult to manage. James was afraid of needles to the point where he would do more than just cry. One time at the family doctor's, when James was to receive an immunization, he was so petrified that he bolted out of the office and ran all the way home. He arrived there before we arrived there by car! James really worked himself up into a tizzy on the day he was to receive an EKG and blood work. Now, James was large and strong for his age, and he was in such emotional straits that he tried to pull the front seat out of our Dodge Caravan and throw it out the sliding door while I was driving up Interstate 95. Fortunately he did not succeed. I was so afraid he was going to hurt himself. He was totally out of control, and by the time we had completed the tests, I was exhausted and very anxious. Once the procedures were over, he returned to his normal self.

In middle school, James never wanted to get out of bed for school. He wasn't scared to go to school; he just wanted to stay in bed. Having to deal with this issue every morning was very distressing. He did not respond to being called multiple times or touched on the arm to wake him. Neither an alarm clock nor *The 1812 Overture* played at a very loud volume would budge him! Eventually, his diagnosis was changed to ADHD with oppositional defiant disorder. Cooperation was not part of his vocabulary.

He did marginally well in school, and I was always trying to help him. Sometimes it felt like I was going to school again. He was evaluated by an outside psychiatrist and put into a special classroom with his own individual educational plan. My husband would come to the sessions when James's IEP was discussed, but he did not participate in counseling, homework, or anything else that had to do with his disorder. My husband saw his job as the manager of the boys' hockey teams. Here again, Arthur was the good cop because he had fun with the boys while they practiced and played hockey. I was the bad cop, doing the heavy lifting with the management of the boys' behavioral issues.

Eventually, James bonded with several other kids, most of whom had similar issues. They loved playing hockey together and going to each other's houses. They were not bad kids, but when they got together it was necessary to monitor what they were doing. I must confess I was not happy when one of the boys punched a hole in the wall of a room we had just finished building in the basement.

During middle school, James rode home on the school bus with his sister. Twice in one week, he attempted to choke her because he wanted to show off for his friends. James thought he was being funny, but Song became very upset and was traumatized by his behavior. To this day, she has not forgiven him, nor does she have a relationship with him. Basically she does not trust him—and who can blame her?

The older James got, the more difficult he became. When we moved to Massachusetts, he got more and more out of control. Additionally, he would make friends and then abandon them. He tried to work at McDonald's but got fired when he peed in the soap dispenser. He was on the hockey team in his high school, and Arthur and I would go to some of the games, but he was always benched the entire game. He was allowed to practice but not allowed to play. He never told us why, although we asked. We ultimately found out that he was smoking, which the coach forbade. In February, he quit the hockey team, and we could not blame him—he was always benched. He also tried to organize a full-scale walkout at school for no specific reason. The administration got wind of his intentions and threatened to suspend him. Fortunately he reconsidered after my husband and I desperately tried to reason with him.

He was having a rather difficult time in school, although he was in special education and put into support classes, which he did not take advantage of. Part of his difficulty with school, and life in general, was dealing with authority figures and making good decisions. While we were still living in Massachusetts, Arthur and I took James to a counselor who wrote the following comment: "James has come to counseling to learn to cope with authority figures (parents/teacher) and to make better decisions for himself. Obviously the event that brings him before the court that he continued to have lapses of judgment … James is a very bright young man. He has many talents and abilities that are clouded by his behavioral problems."

James barely graduated from high school, with mostly Cs and Ds. After that, he wanted to go to a community college about fifty miles from our home. He was driving at that point, and so we asked him to look for a place to stay close to the college. He found some other guys to live with, but the house was less than desirable and the kids essentially destroyed the things we gave them. We asked James to get a small job just to pay for his food. (Actually, he was always coming home and clearing out our pantry.) During the spring semester, he finally landed a job as a groundskeeper for a golf club, which he really enjoyed.

Unfortunately, he was becoming more and more argumentative, irrational, and demanding; he could not finish his freshman year because he was too psychotic to take his exams, although he liked his courses. His behavior got worse over the summer, becoming more and more out of control, with truly crazy thinking. For instance, he would cover his TV whenever people talked to him. Once that summer, when he was really out of control, his father and I convinced him that he needed to be evaluated in the outpatient psychiatric unit. I took him to the hospital where I worked, and he was there for about eight hours, with a discharge diagnosis of mania secondary to his medications. Unfortunately, they released him—even though he was escorted out of the hospital by security. I must admit I was very disappointed. Shortly after that, on September 10, 2001, he had his first diagnosed psychotic break—he was very delusional and paranoid—and was hospitalized. He was diagnosed with bipolar disorder. He believes to this day that 9/11 would not have happened if he had not been in the hospital. He was still very sick when he was discharged. He hated taking his medication.

At home, James would hole up in his room and play video games until the wee hours of the morning. He was always on my work laptop, so I barely had access to it. One early morning before Arthur and I left for work, the CIA showed up at our door. To say the least, we were surprised. Unbeknownst to us, James had been sending e-mails to Jenna Bush. Of course the CIA was concerned about her safety and wanted to make sure that James was not a threat to her. We assured the agents that he was not.

Most of the time, James was benign, but when he was psychotic, he would become violent, and Arthur and I were afraid to be in our own home. Arthur slept with a rather heavy baseball bat next to his side of the bed, because we were so afraid of James's unpredictable behavior. We had at least six restraining orders taken out on him during his lifetime. He landed in the state mental hospital forensic unit twice, for six-month stints. We always tried to support him and visit him while he was in the hospital, but he often responded angrily and would even fling food at me. He was admitted to several other hospitals and had many outpatient care providers, each of whom he fired. He rarely took the medicine prescribed for him, and he would try to convince the psychiatrist that he had ADD and needed more Dexedrine. Unwittingly, the psychiatrist would prescribe Dexedrine in the amounts that James said he needed. Then James would take the amount of Dexedrine he wanted and sell the rest. This was a very lucrative business.

The Dexedrine made James very psychotic, but he did not realize this. His psychosis would manifest itself as mood swings, hallucinations, increased excitement, hostility, aggression, and paranoia. As he got older, James began drinking alcohol as well, exacerbating his psychosis.

There were times when the courts or James's treatment team would assign me to dispense his medication. This was a disaster, because when I would give it to him, he would throw it back at me. There was nothing I could do; he was like a wild man. This was particularly true if he was prescribed an antipsychotic like Zyprexa, which made him ravenous. I could not tell if the Zyprexa was beneficial, because he never took it on a regular basis. His treatment team tried to work with him, but he was impossible.

One time when James was in a psychiatric hospital, I received a phone call at work from one of his social workers, who recommended that I take a class for caretakers of schizophrenic patients. "Is there something you forgot to tell me?" I asked. "I was under the impression that James is bipolar. Are you telling me he is schizophrenic?" The response from the social worker was yes. It was during this hospital stay that James insisted we were in collusion with the federal government, the Secret Service, and the social security system—and laundering money on the side.

I could go on and on about some of the delusions and psychotic events James has had. He is well known to the CIA and the FBI. He was well known to the police in the town where we lived in Massachusetts.

It makes me sad to think about the hell he has been through, and the hell my family has been through, due to his mental illness. Bipolar with psychosis or paranoid schizophrenic—whatever his diagnosis, it is a serious illness and life altering to the patient and those around him.

For instance, on several occasions James was stopped by police and put into a holding cell. This always led to a call in the middle of the night informing us of his whereabouts, to which Arthur would respond, "How long can he stay there?" Arthur and I would take our time getting to the police station the next day. Arthur's intent was to let James suffer a little and perhaps realize the cause of his incarceration. I, on the other hand, was a softie. I lacked the spirit of revenge; instead I nurtured a spirit of forgiveness and empathy. In retrospect, I'm not sure either of us handled such situations correctly.

James is now thirty-five years old and until recently had a wonderful girlfriend who is fifty-seven. She told me that James did not appreciate anything she helped him with and that she was going to leave. She had better control over him than I did, I think in part because he was taking some of his medications. But he wasn't taking all of them because they affect his sex life, which has always been extremely significant to him. Underneath this crazy person, there is a sweet guy who is tender and loving. He always appreciates whatever I do for him. I dearly love him, and I hope and pray that he can maintain the life he has been living for several years. I know he is still delusional and psychotic at times, and I have learned not to argue with him. I simply leave the situation, protecting myself physically and mentally by setting boundaries. I told James's girlfriend that her safety came first, and that I was very grateful for her involvement in his life.

Being mentally ill has caused James to lose friends, which is both sad and isolating. He was trying to keep his financial life together by selling flags on the side while making sure he stayed within the limitations of legal disability. I have cried a lot over the sweet son I lost to mental illness. I know that I am not alone in this situation;

there are many parents with mentally ill children, and their situations are heartbreaking and also scary, because the illness can result in unpredictable and dangerous behaviors. My heart bleeds with theirs, as I know the pain they have gone through. Mental illness is no minor problem for the patient and his or her family.

Song was the least complicated of our children. She and I were glued to the hip from the start, I think in part because she did not know her father in Korea. To this day, we have an awesome relationship. It is true when I tell you that we've had one—yes, just one—argument in our lives. She was acting like a spoiled teenage brat, and I called her a bitch. Never before or since have I called her anything but Peanut, Sweetheart, Honey, or Dear. She was truly a gift sent to us from God, and lately she has been my guardian angel. I don't know what I would have done without her. She has been there for me, and I have been there for her.

Song was a very smart child. We got her when she was two years, three months old, and by the time she was two and a half, she understood everything we said to her. She also spoke fairly well. She was a delightful child to have around. There is one Korean word I learned and kept in reserve, and that is *anio*, which means "no." I vowed to myself that I would use this word only in critical situations such as Song putting her hand on the stove, which she never did. Then, on the day of her baptism, wearing the beautiful white dress her godmother had purchased for her, she was playing with her friends and some other kids who'd come to her party and she stuck a pebble up her nose. After removing the pebble, I told her, "Anio!" and she burst into tears. Clearly she remembered the word, and who knows what else came to her mind.

By the age of three, Song was telling me what she would and wouldn't wear. This was and still is a very frustrating aspect of her personality. When parachute pants and jogging suits were in fashion, Song would wear her old, favorite outfits day after day rather than some of the fashionable ones I had selected for her from a nice department store. This behavior turned out to be fortuitous.

As they are to many girls, friends were important to Song. She would spend a lot of time playing with her girlfriends, and she loved to attend and have sleepovers. She also loved animals, especially cats. As she got older, she learned to ice skate and joined some symmetric ice skating teams. She really was a sweet child.

When she was in elementary school, she had learning issues. Apparently she could not track words or sentences with her eyes. We were referred to an amazing therapist, Dr. Louis Pica, who suggested that we take an experimental course jointly offered by the University of Pennsylvania and Children's Hospital of Philadelphia. This course offered clear learning strategies and appropriate limits for how long children should be spending on their homework, based on their age and grade. In eight weeks, Song advanced two grade levels in reading and arithmetic. We were encouraged to keep a journal/communication book with the teacher, which we did, and this too was very beneficial. Song received academic support throughout elementary school. One special education teacher Song was particularly fond of, Ms. Jean, also had an animal sanctuary, and she would invite her students to visit it.

Song did fairly well in middle and high school. If you ask her today, she will tell you that if she had studied in high school like she did in college, she would have been valedictorian! After high school she was accepted at Moore College of Art and Design in Philadelphia. She graduated with honors with a major in fashion and a minor in textiles. Today, at the age of thirty-two, she is a full-fledged designer of women's sweaters and has worked for a number of high-end design companies. She is married to a wonderful man with whom I have a great relationship ... we both are Capricorns! And she now is an awesome mother of a toddler, who is also a very sweet child.

It was the synchronization of many of these family problems that I was trying to deal with—often unsuccessfully, because there is no cure for the illnesses James has and the ones Arthur had—that ultimately took its toll on me. I was genetically primed to have mental illness, and the many crises in my life then exacerbated what was initially labeled as major depression and anxiety disorder. I tried to help each of my family members with their particular problems, which in James's case was often frustrating because of a lack of cooperation or, to state it better, a lack of insight on the part of Arthur and James. With Edward, my frustration and anger resulted from his lack of respect for me as a person. I am certain I was not the best mother in the world—although I certainly did try my best—because there were many days I could not get off the couch or out of bed. I was often very sad, and my children were too young to realize what was going on with me, though they came to see me in the hospital almost every night during my first hospitalization. I am sure this was not what they wanted to do on their summer evenings! Although I tried to be there for them, I realize now that I was not. And how could I have been, when I was just trying to stay alive? I am sure my illness had a negative impact on their lives, and for that I am very, very sorry. In all honesty, I did my best to take care of myself so that I would get better. I always did everything I was told to do by my doctors and therapists, although I suffered many negative side effects from drugs and ECT. I did not abuse my children, and I always tried to protect them the best I could, but clearly I was not always there for them. I hope they can forgive me in their hearts. To this day I try my best to be there for them, but I have learned that I cannot do this at my emotional or physical expense. If I overextend myself, I pay for it by being very tired the next day, as the chronic fatigue I gained along the path of healing has yet to abate.

Chapter 8

The Evolution of Major Depression and Subsequent Diagnoses

*A*s an adult, I learned that I had suffered a lot of trauma—physical, emotional, mental, and sexual abuse—when I was a child. Though I certainly wasn't the most mistreated child on the face of the earth, the sum of those singular events compounded and eventually affected me significantly.

You might think I would have learned my lesson about working too hard in high school, but I clearly hadn't taken that thinking to its logical conclusion. I was one of those teenagers who thought she knew it all, but I didn't. I was stubbornly convinced at the time that working myself to the point of collapse was right and necessary. Actually, no one tried to intervene while I was in the process of driving myself to such an extreme, and no one tried to help me understand what I was doing to myself. I didn't realize the danger of burning the candle at both ends. In retrospect, I see that working too hard became a lifelong problem for me because it was an essential quality for maintaining status within my family. In other words, I learned from the best! In fact, it was my stubbornness and my own lack of insight that destroyed my goals and contributed to my stress, my suicidal moments, my self-isolation, my loss of memory, and my limited outside interests.

But there was help along the way, such as the Price family, who despite my agnostic leanings propped me up with their true Christianity; Dr. Dave A., who was always upbeat and encouraging; and poor Chris, with whom I spent hours during our stay at the university, and whose memory and eventual suicide still affect me deeply today.

In 1977, Arthur and I met, and this changed my mood quite a bit; up till then I had considered myself unlovable, and I had never understood the concepts of being loved and loving myself. Oddly enough, I also thought of myself as undesirable because I have very heavy legs that aren't at all shapely. At last I began to realize that the psychological damage I had suffered during my first twenty-six years of life had deterred me from perceiving myself as a lovable person. Though I seldom dated in high school or college, the two relationships I *did* consider as having marriage potential turned out to be gay and platonic. I never considered the few men I dated after college to be marriage material, I think because a certain part of me feared being rejected and hurt. But when I met Arthur, something between us clicked. Though he was Catholic (I had never dated a Catholic before), I knew on the first date that I wanted to marry him, and I became a happier person with Arthur because someone actually loved me. The "love" I'd experienced earlier, such as the love of my father, had damaged my trust, but as my sense of caution lessened, I learned to trust Arthur's love to the point that I saw in him the potential for marriage and children. Oddly enough, the more fulfilled I felt, the more my faith in God returned. I suppose being surrounded by Roman Catholics was part of God's divine plan for me. The darkness of my life began to change to shades of gray.

I mentioned earlier that as a child I really didn't know how to play.

According to my shaman, a spirit entered my body when I was about five years old and instilled in me the inability to play or develop an imagination. When I look back on my life, this assessment seems oh so true, for I really didn't understand how to make believe, something little kids usually engage in when they are at play.

During our marriage, Arthur was frequently sick, requiring my nursing abilities and skills. He was often in need of intravenous antibiotics, about which I was very knowledgeable. One of the things I did for myself at the time was take a cake-decorating class. Not only was it a lot of fun, but it also enabled me with a helpful skill. I also did some needlework, such as cross-stitching, needlepoint, and candle wicking. I had always engaged in various crafts when not working at my job or attending to household chores or the family in general. On occasion, usually after the kids went to bed, I would sit with my husband, doing crafts, while he watched television. In retrospect, I realize how little time I took for myself in comparison to the time I spent attending to everyone else's needs.

I felt that the household tasks should have been divided differently, but with the word *no* being absent from my vocabulary, I was at a loss as to how to solve this problem. As my family members got older, my requests to Arthur and the boys for help went unheeded. Song alone always came to my assistance as a teenager. In fairness, I must admit that Arthur would help when the spirit moved him, but I was otherwise viewed as the doormat—and I allowed it to happen. Parity in our marriage was nonexistent, and I was frequently angered—in fact outraged—by the feeling that I was carrying the major burdens of family, house, laundry, lawn, shopping, ironing, teaching, nursing, mothering, and being a wife. I was often made to feel that it was my responsibility to carry the heavier load because my job didn't pay as much as Arthur's and was therefore less important. But since things needed to be done, and since there was no one else to tackle them, I continued in the same vein. Eventually I employed a cleaning lady, and my son Edward and his friend Brad helped cut the grass, but that was later in life, when Edward was fifteen. At times I considered divorce, but that was something I really did not want to do—for in spite of it all, I truly loved Arthur. But I was aware that my family thought of me as being there for their benefit, and that knowledge had a profound effect on me as I grew older. My life began to get heavy and dark again, but more from repressed anger than from depression; it's been said that anger and depression are opposite sides of the same coin. Since my anger was turned inward, I became a master at swallowing my own point of view and actually found it difficult to both access and express. During this period of my life, I wasn't even certain what was actually happening.

As the years passed, the onslaught of larger problems with Arthur's health and the multiple disconcerting issues presented by our maturing children, especially the boys, took their toll on me. These issues required a considerable amount of my time and attention, and when compounded by my earlier depressive events and my full workload, they spelled imminent emotional disaster.

I was particularly frustrated by Arthur's dismissal of my healthcare recommendations. Despite his diabetes, he continued to consume half-gallons of ice cream, bottles of Coca-Cola, and gallons of whole milk, enjoying the things that were unhealthy for him. Because of his high blood sugar, he had to urinate frequently, and he was unabashed by his choice of places to do so—often the side of a building, if the store or motel would not let him use their facilities. Often he would become arrogant and say to the clerk, "Where do *you* go to the bathroom?" which of course both frustrated and embarrassed me. I often had to remind myself of the wry observation made by my former employer, Dr. Samuels: "You can lead a horse to water, but you cannot make him piss in the trough." But in serious retrospect, I can see that these situations often impacted my health. The many unsettled issues I faced on the home front, the abuse I endured as a child, the stress of working full-time, and the fact that I was genetically primed to have mental health issues.

Nevertheless, despite all these issues, my faith in God was restored—mostly by God's grace and partly by my own effort. Having attended Episcopal church as a child, I realized that there were many commonalities between being Episcopalian and being Catholic. I joined my husband and children in the Catholic Church because that was my obligation as Arthur's wife. When Song was three, I went to the director of religious education at our church and said that I would like to set up a childcare program for three-year-olds. She gave me some religious educational materials, which I included in the curriculum. There were twenty-six children and three teachers who shared responsibility for leading the classroom. The program proved to be both inspirational for me and a welcome addition to the church.

I would attend Mass after taking care of the three-year-olds and find the priest's homilies on target and satisfying. I believe it was God who brought about my conversion to Catholicism. I was also profoundly influenced by my husband's faith; by Father McGee, a weekend associate at our church who worked and taught in Philadelphia and is now a pastor in a large church in North Carolina; Father Gigliotti, another weekend associate and a teacher at a high school in Bucks County, Pennsylvania, who was my private religious tutor and is now associate pastor at a large Catholic church in Sarasota, Florida; Father John Crossin, my husband's playpen friend and our personal family priest; Father Connolly, the associate pastor at our church in New Jersey who is now pastor at the same Sarasota church as Father Gigiliotti; and Father Charles Sheer, a former priest who chose the married life and whom my husband met when he went to Textile University at the Newman Center. I was positively influenced by all these people, and by the Donnelly family and my relatives (especially my mother), who were particularly religious and spirited individuals. I believe that God brought together an army of people for me to see His divine hand at work. These were the people who prayed for me, inspired me, and held me up. These were the people whom God chose to carry me through what was to come in the future—especially Father Gigliotti who would write letters (and continues to do so) whenever I needed some spiritual direction. Around 1987, I converted to Catholicism and was very happy that I did so. I believe that by my taking this step, our family was more religiously unified; it was a move I came to see as an important one on my part. Furthermore, finding my own religious faith would ultimately play an important role in balancing my life—something I didn't know when I converted.

It was about this time that my dear friend Chris, from the university days, committed suicide. During the same period of time, my son James began to manifest attention deficit hyperactivity disorder and oppositional defiant disorder. Meanwhile my husband's adult-onset diabetes necessitated his use of insulin, even as he remained determined to continue consuming unimaginable quantities of ice cream and Coca-Cola. Although my spiritual life was blossoming and becoming stronger, my faith life was demanding greater expectations of me. Meanwhile I continued to get promotions at work, which led to my being assigned to organize the first health fair at the Burlington Mall—which meant even more work. The fair went well, but the stress of all these combined events was quietly taking its toll on me, something I was unaware of at the time. I honestly thought I was capable of doing all these things at the same time—a foolish mentality for which I had trained myself.

By the winter of 1988, I began having severe headaches—probably from stress, but manifesting as migraines. My doctor prescribed beta-blockers, but these precipitated depression-like symptoms, a common side effect of the drugs. Of course I continued to do what was expected of me in all areas of my life, which of course made the headaches persist. Over the next six months, my depression deepened but I failed to recognize it. I went to a neurologist who prescribed a variety of medications, including tricyclic antidepressants and neuro-stimulation, but nothing worked to alleviate the headaches. In fact they intensified. Finally in May 1989, I was admitted to the hospital where I was working. There I had a CAT scan of my head, which didn't reveal any neurological abnormalities, but I was eventually placed on Prozac, a psychotropic drug that was new at the time. It didn't help the headaches either; instead it caused urinary retention, an anticholinergic effect, and thus I was catheterized while being in the hospital for ten days. (My mother, mother-n-law and my mother's helper, Christine took care of the children and my husband.) When I was taught how to do self-catheterization, I cried and cried, wondering how this could be happening to me—a nurse and a supermom.

I was resting in bed when the resident psychiatrist bustled through the door of my hospital room, and for reasons I can't clearly remember, I said, "I'm sorry." The first words out of his mouth were, "You're an abused person, and you have depression." I was stunned and confused: I had never spoken to or even met him! This instant diagnosis left me totally befuddled. True, I had had a difficult childhood, but I'd never considered myself abused. I'd assumed that the depression and lingering sadness I felt in college stemmed from feelings of being unlovable and overworked. In my distorted thinking, I believed depression was something that happened to people who were less successful, faithful, or caring than I was. I was angry at this stranger who had barged into my world, telling me I was abused and depressed, when the only words I had spoken were "I'm sorry!"

Shortly thereafter, I was discharged from the community hospital, but I continued to take a maintenance dose of Prozac despite needing to catheterize myself at least four times a day. I also continued to be troubled by the doctor's abrupt diagnosis, for I believed I merely had significant headaches of some unknown origin that had nothing to do with depression. Of course, such thinking was skewed.

A few days after being discharged, I found myself unable to get out of bed and ready for work. It was as if I were suffering paralysis bordering on catatonia. Still in denial of what was really happening, I decided that I needed to see a psychiatrist. After all, I'd seen a neurologist for six months without success, and my internist had totally worked me up and found no medical reason for my headaches other than his discharge diagnosis of depression. Therefore it seemed useless to consider anyone except a psychiatrist.

Fortunately Arthur was still home, getting ready to go to work. Seeing I was not myself and unable to help myself, he immediately went to the phone and did as I requested. The psychiatrist, in turn, instructed him to get me dressed and bring me to his office at 11:00 a.m. Once we were there, the only thing I can recall the psychiatrist saying was, "Go home and have sex!" I assume he thought this would be exciting and enjoyable and consequently would make me happy. Good little do-bees, we followed the doctor's order—which was, of course, ineffectual. I still felt unable to move. Arthur notified the hospital that I would not be reporting for work, and I stayed home in bed for the rest of the day. It was as though the mattress and I had become one unit. At that instant, I finally knew intellectually that something was seriously wrong psychologically. I also knew that I didn't respect the psychiatrist I'd just seen. Unfortunately, although I was a nurse, psychiatry was not my forte. I knew only one other psychiatrist, and she was one of our neighbors.

Realizing that I needed therapy and medication, I contacted Dr. A. and asked her to see me. Once I was in her office, she advised me that she didn't treat depression, but dealt with patients who suffered from mild anxiety disorders. Nevertheless, she didn't refuse me as a patient, nor did she recommend another psychiatrist who did deal with depression—at least not in the beginning. Being my neighbor, she would stop by my home and ask me to go for walks with her, hoping the exercise would stimulate the endorphins in my brain and make me feel better. She didn't change the medication I was taking but added a low dose of Xanax so I could sleep—a prescription that worked well.

But even though I was getting much-needed sleep, my depression continued to deepen. I returned to work, but even there I felt more and more depressed. Then suicidal thoughts began seeping into my brain. I was sad, but most of all I was afraid of my suicidal ideations. By the time of my next office visit with Dr. A., I was very, very sick, and she advised me to go for evaluation to the local psychiatric hospital in New Jersey, a rather new institution at that time. She added gently that I might have to stay if the admitting psychiatric physician thought I needed to be hospitalized.

A *psychiatric* hospital? How could this be possible? I wasn't crazy—I knew what that was, having done a rotation in a state psychiatric hospital when I was a nursing student. I saw myself as depressed, sad, and suicidal, but not psychotic, bipolar, or schizophrenic. I'd been seeing a therapist, Dr. Williams, because of my son James, and he said my emotional distress might require additional care and treatment—thus indirectly agreeing with Dr. A. Dr. Williams was almost always gentle with me. When I voiced my suicidal thoughts, he would try to help me identify my dysfunctional thinking, help me view the future with hope and expand my coping and problem-solving repertoire. He would also explore my reasons for living. I felt guilty at the thought of ruining the lives of my family members—especially my children—by taking my own life. His comments certainly gave me something to think about despite my deep psychological pain and my desire for relief from all the feelings associated with depression. I was now at the point where I had to take life moment by moment, day by day.

Dr. A. set up an appointment with the admitting physician at the psychiatric hospital. Then she and Arthur escorted me there for evaluation. During the interview with the admitting physician, I confessed that I had constant thoughts of suicide but had never attempted it. I admitted that a voice in my head (more like an audio loop that kept repeating the same message) continually told me to kill myself. I imagine that this or something else I said earned me a spot in the hospital, for an aide was called to the office to escort me to a room. Arthur gave me a hug but never commented on what he thought was going to happen to me.

When the door slammed behind me and I found myself in a locked unit without my husband at my side, I began to cry and shake profusely, ashamed by the whole admission process. I'd been thoroughly strip-searched, which left me feeling like a criminal. I was in a two-bed room with a metal, convex mirror that made seeing yourself almost impossible. Also, for days I was on twenty-four-hour watch in case I attempted to commit suicide. I kept thinking, *Oh god! What have I done now?* Though it seemed like a nightmare, I knew I wasn't imagining it. It was true—I had succumbed to the darkness and despondency of depression.

My admitting diagnosis was major depression with psychosis. *Psychotic?* How could this be true? No doubt the diagnosis stemmed from my admission that I'd heard a voice in my head commanding me to commit suicide.

Two weeks after my admission, Dr. A. came to visit, only to tell me that she was dismissing me as a patient because of the severity of my illness. I started thinking, *Oh god! Can anything else go wrong?* But this was only the beginning of a long series of disappointments and struggles. In spite of being on multiple drug regimens, the hospital psychologist accused me of being a drug addict because I had taken Xanax, when in truth I had taken only what was prescribed for me for sleep. I was silently furious at him, for I knew I was no more a drug addict than the man in the moon. So the Xanax was discontinued and replaced with trazodone, an antidepressant that supposedly helps with sleep. But despite increasingly higher doses, trazodone failed to instill sleep or help with my depression. I would continue lying in my bed, eyes shut, but sleepless. My doctor refused to believe me when I told him that 200 mg of trazadone failed to work for me as a sleep agent.

In reply, he told me to sit in the lounge if I couldn't sleep, which I did night after night.

Meanwhile, since the trazadone wasn't working and I'd been taken off Prozac because of urinary retention, I was prescribed increasingly higher doses of Wellbutrin. But I continued to grow more and more fatigued because of sleeplessness, and my mood steadily declined. At this point I began to experience some strange side effects (presumably from one of the drugs I was taking). At first I was just moderately cold, but by late June I was wearing two fleece-like jogging suits. True, the building was air-conditioned, but the chilliness that I felt was excessive. I began to suspect that the Wellbutrin was the culprit, because the symptoms intensified with each successive dose. I didn't share this suspicion with anyone, however, because I felt that whatever opinions I voiced were seen in the worst possible light, and that people suspected I was not telling the truth. (The fact that I regularly wore two jogging suits in mid-summer should have tipped them off that I really was cold.) Clearly the doctors did not know me or my abhorrence of lying, and they had not had the opportunity to observe the multiple side effects I was experiencing.

Then I began having rigors (shaking chills), started vomiting, and suffered the worst headaches I had ever had—so severe that I felt like my head was splitting down the middle. I called Arthur and told him I was *physically* ill—chilled to the bone, shaking, and unable to keep anything down. I also told my nurse how I was feeling, and he, in turn, had the resident on-call doctor come see me. My husband, meanwhile, called the resident and talked to him, suggesting that I might need medical care beyond what I was receiving at the psychiatric hospital. But the resident told Arthur that I was too psychologically ill to be transferred to a medical facility. What he did do for me was prescribe an antinausea suppository, which my nurse insisted I walk to the desk to get. Furthermore, I was expected to insert the suppository myself, which left me even *less* impressed with the care "provided" by that particular psychiatric nurse. That specific night remains a painful and anxiety-filled memory. I longed for Arthur to be there, to hold me and reassure me, but that was impossible because the prescribed visiting hours were over, and they were strictly enforced.

The following morning, my assigned psychiatrist, Dr. L., dropped by to see me, saying he knew I'd had a terrible night, which seemed to me a ridiculous observation, to say the least. He also said that I'd get better soon, and that, more important, I should *never* allow anyone to prescribe Wellbutrin for me again, because it didn't help the depression and because I also had a toxic drug syndrome, which was in essence a serious adverse reaction to the drug. He added that I didn't have a serotonin syndrome, as I didn't have fever and seizures, but that I needed to wait two weeks for the Wellbutrin to clear from my system so I could start on a monoamine oxidase inhibitor (MAOI), another classification of antidepressants.

In the interim, I was started on Depakote, an antiseizure drug often used as a mood stabilizer for depression. I was given this drug because my mood vacillated. Periodically, out of the blue, I would feel like my normal, healthy self—I was never manic—and this good mood would last for a few days. Then I would feel like I was in the trash can again. I was totally happy when I had those wonderful days, and there seemed to be no particular situation or thinking that precipitated them. The doctors thought the Depakote would help prolong these good periods, so I was placed on that drug for a long time. But except for making me feel totally exhausted and gain weight, it had no beneficial effect on the stability of my mood.

I was also started on Lithobid—a form of lithium salts. Lithium is frequently used for bipolar disorder, and the doctor thought that the variability of my mood and my inability to sleep indicated that I had bipolar depression. Intellectually, that made sense. However, this new diagnosis made me anxious. I was confused: I'd never been manic or hypomanic, and I did not see myself as psychotic. I also began to experience side effects with Lithobid. At first my hands began to shake a little. Then the shaking became excessive; I couldn't write or eat without making a complete mess. Often I would sit on my hands to keep them from shaking. Also, I experienced hypersexuality to such a point that one night, when I had a pass to go out with my husband, I nearly raped him in the car while we were still in the hospital parking lot! The sex was enjoyable, but I knew it wasn't normal. I hadn't cared about sex for *months* because of my headaches and the many antidepressants I'd taken to treat them. (Some antidepressants have the effect of suppressing the libido.) My research indicates that hypersexuality is primarily a function of being bipolar; however, I saw it as a side effect of the Lithobid. And so despite what the doctors were saying, I didn't believe I was bipolar—even if I had one hypersexual episode and my mood was unstable. Fortunately I was taken off the Lithobid, but I remained in the dark, with only an occasional bright day or two.

By now I'd been on several different medications, but none of them worked for me. I still wasn't sleeping well, my mood was still unstable, and in general I was severely depressed. I'd had limited individual psychotherapy during the three months I was in the hospital—maybe four sessions—which seemed odd to me. I was part of an art therapy group and drew several morbid pictures that caused me to lose passes to go outside. For instance, I was supposed to go to a wedding with my husband one particular weekend and had already received a pass. My mother bought me a beautiful new outfit for the occasion, including lovely jewelry, as I had lost a lot of weight between the rigors and the walking, which I did faithfully every day. (In the hospital, there was a centrally located secure area framed by the building's wings, and it was around this square that I walked at least fifty times a day to keep in shape. Also, I was very careful about what I ate. Consequently I lost at least thirty pounds during my three months of hospitalization.)

The week prior to the wedding, our art therapy assignment was to draw a picture of what we were most afraid of. I drew a picture of myself lying in a casket. One the one hand I was afraid of dying; on the other, I was ready to leave the hellish world in which I was living. That honesty—that picture—sealed the deal, and I was forbidden to go to the wedding. Yet I was neither more nor less depressed than I was when I first walked into the hospital.

We also had group therapy, during which we talked about our lives. It was there that I came to realize that I had been emotionally and mentally abused by my father and that my mother had been hypercritical and expected perfection from me. I also realized that the intimate experiences I had shared with my uncle were classified as sexual abuse. These ideas were revelatory and shocking; however, I was not ready to deal with them emotionally, especially not the issue of sexual abuse. (I knew that I disliked my father's behavior, which was why I would not communicate with him for months on end.) I discovered that I'd never had a good self-image and never really loved myself, although I thought of myself as a good person. And I realized that I had worked myself to death during my high school and college years and that my best friends' suicide had profoundly affected my life. I also found myself blaming my mother for not protecting me from my father's emotional abuse, as she would leave me for months at a time to visit her sister in Florida when life got totally unsafe for her. Prior to that realization, I had always been supportive of my mother. The more I recognized the events in my life that had caused me to sink into such deep depression, the darker my life began to look to me.

During my first weeks in the hospital, I was angry with my mother and didn't know what to say to her, so I simply refused to speak to her. My mother and I had always been emotionally bonded; this was the first time I could not talk to her. I realized she had instilled in me a perfectionistic ideal that I was unable to attain. Furthermore, the realization that my mother had not always protected me churned inside me constantly; I couldn't understand how she could have gone off to visit her sister and left Rae and me with our father and then with Nana.

However, about three weeks into my hospital stay, my mother sent me a lovely arrangement of pink roses with baby's breath in a beautiful glass vase decorated with a large pink bow. The nursing staff understandably removed the bouquet from the glass vase and put it in a plastic water pitcher, which of course ruined the beauty of the arrangement, but receiving the flowers from my mother, who was taking care of my children at the time, caused me to burst into uncontrollable sobs. I was at cross-purposes—I felt angry with her but also guilty for feeling that way.

That emotional conflict increased the next day with the arrival of another beautiful arrangement from her (this time a bouquet of pink carnations). Normally respectful and polite, I usually would have had no trouble telling her thank you, but I was in such a state of guilt, remorse, and confusion at the time that I didn't know what to say in acknowledgment of this expression of love and care. Eventually I got myself together and called to thank her. Ultimately the flowers were the icebreaker that reunited us, and I was able to talk to my mother on the phone again. In retrospect, it's easy to see that I was thinking only of my own pain without considering the pain my mother was experiencing, with a daughter who had always been supportive of her now seemingly turned against her. Even today I remain sorry for my self-centered action, and I hope that as time passed, Mom found it in her heart to forgive my selfishness.

Though I could usually forgive almost anyone (except my father) for anything, my ability to forgive had been replaced with excruciating pain, darkness, anger, rage, and selfishness. I was not thinking with my mind or my heart; instead I was reacting to years of repressed pain and trauma caused by my father. The verbal, emotional, and physical abuse my mother endured for years wasn't in my conscious mind either. Presumably this was a result of my dark side taking over, though I'd never considered myself as having one. I thought of myself as *living* in the dark, rather than in the light of life.

Meanwhile I spent weeks clearing my system of the toxic effects of the Wellbutrin. Because the doctor wanted me to start on the MAOI drug Parnate, I had to stop consuming things like cheese (no more pizza), wine (none was served in the hospital), fava beans, and bananas, all of which contain tyramine, which can cause a severe elevation of blood pressure when combined with MAOI drugs. At first I was given only small doses of Parnate, but then the doses were increased little by little. I was still taking Depakote too, but despite the combination, my depressed mood failed to respond. And so my psychiatrist suggested I try electroconvulsive therapy. I'd had a sick feeling that he would suggest ECT, because other patients on our unit had been going from the psychiatric hospital to the local hospital for their ECT treatments, so I knew this would be an option for me too. But having seen these patients return to the psychiatric hospital looking like zombies, and as I personally felt the treatments were barbaric, I told the psychiatrist in no uncertain terms that I would *not* accept ECT treatments.

So after receiving therapeutic doses of Parnate, I was discharged from the hospital eighty-nine days after I entered through its secure doors. I had learned a lot, however, and suicidal thoughts no longer assailed me, although my depression remained severe. I suspect the suicidal thoughts went away because someone was taking care of me for once, and I was no longer the caretaker for myself and my family. At my discharge, I was diagnosed as having a major depressive disorder—*that* after all the tinkering around with other diagnoses!

The hospital staff knew I didn't have a psychopharmacologist, so they sent me to a doctor whose office was more than an hour and a half from my home. This physician would see me for ten minutes at $120 a visit. To his credit, he wanted to see me twice a week upon discovering how deeply depressed I was, but that made life somewhat difficult for us financially; not only did I have to pay the psychopharmacologist $240 a week, but I also owed the psychologist $80 a week, which was a bargain.

All this money was coming out of our pockets, because my outpatient psychiatric coverage had long been used up. (Our medical insurance would pay a total of only $500 for both doctors' fees and medication over the course of a year.)

The psychopharmacologist continued to increase my doses of Parnate, which combined with the Depakote left me perpetually tired. I had to give myself time to rest when scheduling my visits to his office; I'd stop halfway to and from there and sleep in the car. I also began to put on weight, which I wasn't happy about, and I didn't have the energy to take the long walks I'd taken when I was hospitalized.

Realizing we couldn't keep up this financial outlay, I finally located a psychiatrist at a well-known psychiatric hospital in Philadelphia that was closer to our home. Dr. S. charged a lot less than my previous doctor. He took care of me for about six months, continuing me on the same drugs. Once again I began to have headaches.

In May 1990, when I started exhibiting signs of suicide again, he immediately placed me in the Philadelphia facility. I spoke with my therapist, Dr. Williams, who explained that sometimes patients are hospitalized for medication changes. Since I had been on just about every class of psychotropic drug for depression, I was apprehensive about what change was going to be made. When Dr. S. advised me that I needed ECT, the idea frightened me, but I finally consented, knowing there were few options left.

While a patient in this hospital, I attended two therapy groups, opting for the ones that included horticulture and dance. I especially loved working with plants in the hospital's greenhouse, and Rae had given me a lot of silk flowers and materials to make floral arrangements. At the same time, however, I was becoming quite vocal about my suicidal thoughts and feelings, which understandably upset the other patients. So the staff approached me with a deal: I would still be permitted to work with the crafts my sister provided (which included refurbishing some of the hospital's own stale arrangements) if I would no longer verbalize my thoughts about suicide. Needless to say, I bought into the deal.

On the first day of my electroshock therapy, a nurse accompanied me to the outpatient ECT unit. I was put to sleep with a short-acting anesthetic, and then the electrode and shock were applied to the left temporal area. I did not feel anything during the treatment, which activated a seizure. After my treatment, I felt very tired and slept for a long time. However, the afternoon after the *second* ECT, which was administered early in the morning, I danced with a lot of feeling and movement during my dance therapy class. Everyone was impressed by how quickly I responded to the ECT. The headaches and depression subsided, and I felt much happier. Dr. S. wanted to continue with the treatments—I received six while I was an inpatient—but they had to be stopped when I exhibited signs of significant memory loss. For example, after waking up from each treatment, I was asked an orientation question such as "Who is president of the United States?" When my answer was "Nixon," the team knew I was out in left field.

After the treatments were stopped and I was discharged, I continued to see my psychiatrist and psychologist on an outpatient basis. I was thankful the treatments had stopped, for I was having great difficulty remembering how to drive to familiar locations. (I had to call Dr. Williams three weeks in a row to get directions to his office. A gentle person, he graciously gave me directions each time; not until after my third call did it occur to me to write them down.) Also, I always seemed to be searching for words, and I knew I had lost a lot of my nursing knowledge. My husband would joke with me, saying, "It's fun taking you places because you act like you've never been there before." But it wasn't much fun for me!

Research has found that ECT can cause temporary memory loss, but that usually involves the recall of recent information. However, some research reveals more severe memory loss in a very small percentage of people who receive ECT; I apparently qualified for this distinction. In my case, the ECT affected not only my recent memory, but also my long-term memory. So while ECT worked for me, I found that the accompanying memory loss was unacceptable. Furthermore, the happy state I experienced after treatments didn't last—perhaps because I had not had enough of them.

Nevertheless, Dr. S. again recommended ECT when the headaches and sadness returned. So my husband would take me to the hospital's outpatient ECT department in the morning and then pick me up after the treatment and recovery period and take me to the home of my best girlfriend, Lauren. She would remove the electrode glue from my scalp, prepare lunch for me, and make me comfortable so I could rest, for it usually took most of the day to fully recover from a treatment. Not knowing there were new drugs available for my illness, I continued to undergo more ECT with the same post-treatment memory loss. This was very disturbing to me, and the anxiety began affecting my sleep. I called Dr. S. and left him several messages concerning my inability to sleep. After two weeks, he finally returned my calls and recommended chloral hydrate to help me sleep. It had no effect.

It was after a series of outpatient ECT treatments that I attempted to drive to my appointment with Dr. Williams. On this particular day, my mother and I had to drive around and do some errands first. We were using her car that day because mine was being serviced. I stopped by the printer's to pick up some materials while my mother waited in the car and smoked a cigarette. Then I dropped her off, drove down to Dr. Williams's office, rolled up the windows, and locked the car. After my appointment, I went down to the car only to find that there was a green cloud inside. I could not imagine what was going on inside my mother's car, but fortunately I did not open the door. Instead I went upstairs to Dr. Williams's office and asked him to come down and help me sort out the problem. Quickly realizing that the interior of the car was on fire, he called 911. Firefighters arrived and, with a carefully orchestrated series of maneuvers, opened the car door and squirted water inside. The fire was out in minutes, but the interior of my mother's car was completely ruined.

It turned out that when my mother was smoking her cigarette, she had the window open and ashes flew into the backseat. Then, during my appointment with Dr. Williams, the ashes smoldered inside the car. Needless to say, the fire was just one more bit of stress that I did not need when I was already psychologically unglued. A funny postscript to this unfortunate scenario was that it was the impetus for my mother to stop smoking. After more than fifty years, she never had another cigarette.

Besides being upset with Dr. S.'s delay in returning my calls, I had begun to prefer dealing with his partner, Dr. Susan Ulhrich, who had helped with my care while I was in the hospital. She was a straight shooter but compassionate and caring. Furthermore, she was well acquainted with my history and aware that I often felt suicidal. After begging her not to administer any more ECT because of the memory issues, she made a pact with me in the fall of 1990: she would stop the treatments if I would promise to call her whenever I experienced suicidal impulses. She added that it was acceptable to *think* about suicide, but unacceptable to *commit* it. I got the message and agreed to her deal.

It took five years to get most of my memory back and recover from the resultant depression. Little by little, I regained what I had lost, getting to the point where I could at first work part-time and then, later, return to a full-time job. In the interim, I read and read and read, for it was always an adventure to rediscover words I had lost. However, my sense of direction, which was once great, never returned. In those days, GPS's were unavailable, so I had to relearn how to get around. Sometimes I could not find my way out of a paper bag!

I also lost my sense of balance—and it never returned either. Prior to ECT, I was very agile and quite sure-footed. Today when I attempt to do a tree pose in yoga, I have to use a wall for support. Additionally, I have a great propensity for falling, because both my balance and my proprioception were affected by the ECT.

The first time I visited Dr. Ulrich as an outpatient, she prescribed two drugs that were relatively new on the market: Risperdal and Zoloft. The Risperdal was for sleep, and the Zoloft was for depression. With the combination of these two drugs, I was able to sleep at night and my mood temporarily improved. After a few months, however, the Zoloft became ineffectual, and so she switched my antidepressant to a different SSRI (selective serotonin reuptake inhibitor), Paxil. For many years thereafter, I took both Paxil and Risperdal, which were relatively helpful. Of course, these came with their own side effects—decreased libido and weight gain. The Risperdal eventually caused galactorrhea (leakage of milk from my nipples). Doctors eventually stopped the Risperdal because they weren't certain about the long-term effects of galactorrhea. They also stopped the Paxil when I began to crash about thirteen years later. In retrospect, that was a rather long time to have been on those drugs, but they did make me functional enough to work. Unfortunately, the stress connected with family and work was beginning to rule the roost again.

During one of our sessions, Dr. Ulrich began to address the area of sexual abuse with me by recommending a workbook on the subject, with the directive to read it slowly. I had no serious reaction to the book, but one day while I was talking with Dr. Williams, the violation of my body became a harsh reality to me. After leaving his office, I went home, crawled into bed, and cried and cried and cried. I couldn't stop sobbing, thinking of how my uncle had taken advantage of me when I was so young, both physically and emotionally violating me. In recalling that period, I would say it was the only time I grieved over the violation of my body, and it was the only time I experienced a real sense of trauma regarding those incidences of sexual seduction. After that episode, I never spoke to my uncle again. Eventually I had the opportunity to talk about the incident with my cousin Karl, who was surprised but, as a lawyer, respected the attorney-client privilege. I also spoke with my sister about it, and although she suffered no such abuse at the hands of our uncle, she admitted to having been raped by an attendant while in the hospital. Her attacker was subsequently incarcerated after a very difficult and emotional trial.

As a footnote to this whole unsavory family incident, I met my uncle's grandson for dinner about two years ago, and at one point he started discussing our many relatives, pointedly admitting that there was a rumor in the family that one member had been sexually abused by another. He went for the jugular and point-blank asked me if I knew about it. I was reluctant to tell him that I had been the victim of his grandfather, who had recently died, but when I did, he was surprised but also empathetic.

In 1995, I was well enough to get a full-time job at Fox Chase Cancer Center doing data management in the Department of Radiation Oncology. At the same time, my husband secured a job in Watertown, Massachusetts, with a large, well-regarded painting company. This meant that Arthur lived in a Victorian boardinghouse in Waltham, Massachusetts, during the week and returned to New Jersey for the weekends. I was thankful that he made the effort to come home at the end of each week to lend a hand and give me emotional support with the boys. The rest of the time I was home alone with the children, working and trying to sell our house while keeping it in ready-to-show order. The twelve months following Arthur's move to Waltham were filled with considerable stress. Between the summers of 1995 and 1996, both boys grew increasingly out of control and disrespectful toward me. Edward was so rude and disobedient that I went to the office of the Division of Youth and Family Services for some assistance. By court order, Edward was placed in a foster home for three weeks. After that he was happy to be home. In the meantime, James was also revving up, smoking and getting into trouble with his friends. In May 1996, I had to pack the house and move its contents to our new home in Franklin, Massachusetts. I also had to make arrangements for the kids, because school was not over until the end of June. Song was lucky enough to have a friend put her up for that interval, and I was very thankful. I made similar arrangements with one of James's friends. Edward and his girlfriend stayed with me in very low-cost motels. While I was working, Edward got his girlfriend pregnant, unbeknownst to the rest of us. Eating all our meals out and paying for motels and living expenses for James essentially took my entire paycheck each week. All of this was very stressful, but I never became suicidal, even though my anxiety was sky-high. Fortunately I continued my weekly appointments with Dr. Williams, who helped me sort out many of these issues, offering suggestions for managing my family and setting boundaries while taking care of myself. I have no idea what I would have done without him. That whole month and a half was a blur, as I was trying to deal with everyone's situation without the support of my husband.

When our family finally relocated to Massachusetts in June 1996, I had to find a psychopharmacologist because I needed refills of my medication. I had been seeing Dr. Ulrich every three months and had been fairly stable in spite of the stress and anxiety I was feeling. Finding a psychiatrist who took new patients and worked with our insurance was a difficult job. Fortunately, I was able to find Dr. James, who had space in his practice for a new patient. He was an older, very matter-of-fact gentleman who listened as I recited my history, including my medications and their respective side effects. I also said that I considered myself fairly stable despite our many prevailing family issues. He responded that if I needed hospitalization, I would be admitted to his respective hospital.

Things began to get chaotic in our household. Edward was only eighteen when he brought his girlfriend and baby home the following summer, in June 1997. James began to get more paranoid, was having great difficulty in school, and started showing signs of bipolar disorder. I asked Dr. James if I could see a therapist, as I felt that I had lost my ability to communicate with my children. Little did I realize that it was my children who had problems with communication.

In 2001, James was diagnosed with bipolar disorder. He was subsequently hospitalized several times, and twice he spent six months in the state mental hospital forensic unit. Around 2003, Robin, the mother of Edward's son, Nathan, secretly took him away to the Southwest. This was traumatic for the entire family, but especially so for Edward and me. I had lost my grandson and had no idea when, if ever, I would see him again. Fortunately, Edward hired a private investigator who located Robin and Nate. The courts insisted that Nathan be returned to Edward in Massachusetts. Robin was also ordered to return to Massachusetts and stay there.

In 2003, my husband had his leg amputated, and in 2004, all of the foregoing events, plus the stress of my job, caught up with me. My office manager suggested I go to the Employee Assistance Program (EAP) provided by the well-known hospital where I worked. The helpful counselors at the EAP steered me in the right direction, suggesting I get a restraining order on James (Arthur and I had already taken out several), change our locks, install an alarm system, and arm ourselves with pepper spray or any comparable device. They also suggested I see Dr. Holly, a therapist. By then Dr. James had retired, and by the grace of God I ran into James's psychiatrist, and so I asked her to recommend another psychopharmacologist. She told me about Dr. Dave. Both Dr. Holly and Dr. Dave made time for me whenever a crisis arose.

When I went to see Dr. Holly in April 2004, I was an emotional wreck—totally stressed, my mood beginning to slip, and my grip on life loosening. I had puttered along for years, taking one day at a time, simply hanging in there. The joke between us was "How many fingers are you holding on with?" I had a pattern of two weeks of grace and two weeks of chaos; I felt like I was on a perpetual roller coaster. This pattern, validated by Dr. Holly, had been in place for many, many years. Rather than learning from each event, however, I would descend further into a hole of depression with each successive difficult situation, and I become exhausted attempting to climb out. There was hardly time to recover from one event or rationally deal with it before another overwhelming problem presented itself. Consequently there was rarely a respite during which I could sort out a proper solution.

In 2006, Arthur died. While I was thankful that he was no longer suffering, I was very sad and I dearly missed him. James's problems were looming larger and larger, and my mother now required my constant care. That was also the year that Edward threatened to take Nathan away from me, which led to the first of my four hospitalizations over the next several years.

During my first hospitalization at a Harvard-affiliated hospital, I was labeled with bipolar II. I've never understood how they came up with that diagnosis, because the criteria include hypomanic episodes (hypomania is less severe than mania, often characterized by symptoms of increased activity, racing thoughts, the need for decreased sleep, delusions of grandeur, and elevated mood) lasting at least four days (which I hadn't had in recent years); depressive episodes (of which I had plenty); and a full-blown manic episode (which I'd never had). The depressive episodes are more frequent and last longer than hypomanic episodes or intervals of well-being (this was true of me). Also, bipolar II is associated with a greater risk of suicidal thoughts and behaviors than unipolar depression or bipolar I (this was also consistent with my experience). At any rate, after I was discharged, I spoke with Dr. Dave, telling him I was upset with the diagnosis. But he reaffirmed that I had major depression and definitely did not have bipolar II. So I lived with the diagnosis of major depression for the next year and a half.

I have always been plagued by severe, relentless anxiety. It seemed to me that the anxiety piggybacked on the depression, and sometimes it was so intense that I was afraid of being by myself for fear of suicidal ideations. Consequently I paid my friend Cady to stay with me on weekends, because my children were unavailable to do so. Occasionally I would take a bus to New York City to stay with my daughter, who lived and worked there with her husband. A change in venue was helpful, as were the compassionate care and attention provided by my daughter and husband. There in New York, I was out of my element and not worrying about everything occurring in and around me.

This episode of severe anxiety persisted for nearly a year. I was unaware how significant it was until years later, when I read the journals that I had diligently kept for many years. Not only did the journals serve as a useful point of reference for this memoir, but it was also therapeutic using them to track my mood and the events that altered it and increased my anxiety. Fortunately my psychiatrist prescribed Klonopin, which helped control the anxiety.

One day during a routine office visit, Dr. Dave asked me if I ever wrung my hands. The answer was a resounding "Yes! I do it at every stoplight when I am driving." To this day I continue to wring my hands at traffic lights and stop signs. This is a subconscious behavior, and I have made a conscious effort to stop, but it still continues. Given this tidbit of information, along with other symptoms I exhibited, Dr. Dave changed my diagnosis from major depression to agitated depression. He told me that agitated depression is close to being bipolar. As was my habit, I looked up the symptoms of agitated depression, and once again I didn't like what I read. The classic symptoms include feelings of irritability, anger and agitation, all mixed at the same time with mania and depression, danger of self-injury, fatigue, guilt, impulsiveness, irritability, morbid or suicidal ideations, panic or paranoia, and pressured speech. Rage occurs at the same time. Tearfulness occurs during manic episodes. These may be accompanied by feelings of being a failure, flight of ideas, auditory hallucinations, confusion, insomnia, delusions of persecution, restlessness, or feelings of worthlessness. Habitual pacing may also be present. Understandably, this is a difficult form of depression to treat; it is also referred to as mixed states of depression. I didn't think I had most of these symptoms.

Of course, I am not a doctor and I do not pretend to know all of the classifications of the DSM-V, the reference book that classifies modern psychological disorders. But one thing was clear: my depression, no matter how it was labeled, truly was difficult to treat, as it seemed unresponsive to all classic treatments. I had been on all types of medication and had received many ECT treatments, but none of them controlled my depression for a sustained period of time with the exception of the combination of Paxil and Risperdal. I'd been on various combinations of drugs over the previous eleven years: Remeron, Lexapro, Cymbalta, Benadryl, Seroquel, Klonopin, vitamin D, Xanax, Ativan, Abilify, Lamictal, and Provigil. During my years of depression, I'd been on twenty-eight different medications in varying combinations. The reality is, there is no guarantee that one medication or combination of medications will work; it's all trial and error. One unfortunate thing about using prescribed drugs is that it often takes several weeks to achieve a therapeutic dose and determine its effectiveness. This means that a severely depressed patient needs to be monitored carefully while the effectiveness of the prescribed drug is determined. In severe suicidal situations, ECT may be required to get the patient through the most acute phase of depression.

As I mentioned previously, I've experienced significant side effects to many of the drugs. For example, I had an adverse reaction to Lamictal, which worked well but produced a rash, a potentially dangerous symptom. Remeron seemed to cause agitation and mania. A ubiquitous side effect of many drugs is weight gain. I had gained so much weight by 2005 that I had gastric bypass surgery and subsequently lost a *lot* of weight. However, during the past ten years, I've gained back more than half of it, which hasn't made me happy. This, however, is a reality that I have had to accept and work on. Constipation is another common side effect; I deal with it by taking stool softeners and gentle laxatives, including vegetables, fruits, and fiber-containing substances.

While my diagnosis of agitated depression had remained the same for a long period of time, my doctor also thought I was struggling with grief. Not only had I lost a lot of people in my life over a short period of time, but I had also lost my job, my self-confidence, some of my memory again from the more recent ECT treatments, and my son James to schizophrenia. My friend Kay, from the widow's group to which I belong, had been to a grief counselor after she lost her husband, and stated, "It was the best investment in myself I ever made." So I sought out a grief counselor. He decided that I had enough people in my "village" taking care of me and didn't need one more. He recommended that either my therapist or my psychiatrist help me deal with my grief instead. After a few months of routine therapy, neither my counselor nor my psychiatrist had initiated grief counseling, and so I asked my psychiatrist, Dr. Dave, if he would consider taking me on as a therapy patient. He said he would consider it, and on my next visit he agreed. I'd decided that no matter the financial cost, it would be worth it if I got better. As it turned out, Dr. Dave was very helpful. The more we talked, the less he believed I had major depression, deciding instead that I had complicated grief, PTSD, anxiety, and agitated depression.

Unlike other diagnoses, this set made sense to me. I had experienced a lot of grief, trauma, and anxiety in my life. What had confused everyone over the prior twenty or so years was the fact that the symptoms of grief, PTSD, and anxiety are similar to those of major depression. Dr. Dave and I met every week for a while and then every two weeks. Today we meet once a month. In the midst of this intensive therapy, both my regular therapist, Dr. Holly, and my group therapist, Geri, said I was making a lot of progress. Both counselors thought I was gaining emotional strength, dealing with situations better, setting limits on the needs of family members, and liking and caring for myself better. Gradually I was gaining more energy, although the chronic fatigue and insomnia continued unless I was heavily medicated.

Chapter 9

Thoughts, Feelings, and Behaviors Associated with My Mental Illness

*I*f you are reading this book, chances are you've had a mental illness or you know someone who has. As I mentioned, I've had a variety of diagnoses, many of which share common thought patterns, feelings, and behaviors. Not everyone with grief, anxiety, depression, or post-traumatic stress disorder experiences the exact same set of thoughts, feelings, and behaviors. I've learned in cognitive behavioral therapy that our thoughts usually drive our feelings and subsequently our behaviors. Almost everyone is born with a common set of emotions. However, not everyone reacts with the same set of behaviors. Healthy people often experience all these feelings, just not to the same degree as a mentally ill person. Neither do all mentally healthy people behave the same way. They might dwell on their negative thoughts and feelings for an hour or two, or perhaps a day or two, after which they return to their normal, healthy state. It is the subset of mentally unhealthy people who maintain exaggerated expressions of these thoughts, feelings, and behaviors for days, weeks, months, years, or even a lifetime.

Feelings that are common to most of us include happiness, sadness, fear, anger, trust, anxiety, loneliness, pleasure, love, a sense of belonging, hope, faith, hurt, depression, confusion, interest, and strength. I've experienced all these feelings with varying degrees of intensity. Although in the following pages I generally address behaviors associated with negative feelings, I've experienced all the positive feelings as well.

Sometimes I've felt such extreme sadness, rejection, anger, loneliness, anxiety, fear, and hopelessness that I wanted to die, either from natural causes or suicide. I've even prayed that I would die so that I wouldn't have to endure the pain of those intense, seemingly unremitting negative or damaging feelings. I've been so lonely at times that I've had people stay with me to distract me so that I wouldn't continually contemplate suicide. Other times I've had such a strong desire to end my life that I've needed people around me to prevent my doing harm to myself. It seems I often resorted to anxiety, depression, and suicidal thoughts when I could no longer cope with the multiplicity of problems at hand.

After my fourth hospitalization, when my suicidal ideations were very strong, I had frequent conversations about them with my doctors. Although it was always difficult for me to admit that I felt suicidal, I knew it was in my best interest to share my feelings with them, especially when I began to feel unsafe. My doctors would then attempt to negotiate with me, giving me a chance to improve my thinking rather than hospitalizing me immediately. Sometimes these conversations ended with this admonition: "If you're not better by our next appointment, we'll need to hospitalize you." One of the admonitions they used that forced me to reevaluate my thinking involved guilt, or at least I saw it that way. For example, I interpreted Dr. Williams' admonitions in terms of guilt and that I would ruin the lives of my family members if I committed suicide, and Dr. Ulrich continued to repeat her mantra, "It is acceptable to *think* about suicide and make plans to do so, but it is *not* acceptable to carry them out." When I shared some of my plans with Dr. Dave, he told me how miserable I'd feel if I survived them and caused other inadvertently involved people to suffer unwarranted guilt. He added that suicide is the act of placing the burden of our pain on those we love. Therefore, guilt became a very strong deterrent for me, helping me not follow through on my suicidal plans. I certainly didn't want to ruin the lives of my husband and children or anyone else, no matter how deep my sadness was. I also recognize that suicide is contrary to my Catholic faith, although I firmly believe that God would still love and forgive me if I did commit suicide.

Although I had strong and frequent suicidal thoughts, my practice was to try to push my way through them and, if necessary, call my doctor for help. I could fully anticipate when I needed to be hospitalized, and this became a joint decision with my treatment team. I was never "pink-slipped"—that is, hospitalized involuntarily.

I've been depressed or sad the majority of my life. The more difficult life became, the more I tried to do what was prescribed for me. Rarely did I miss a therapy appointment, a doctor appointment, a group session, an ECT treatment, or a dose of medication. Only during one period in our married life, when there wasn't enough money for medication, did I forego it. (The mentally ill have always been the redheaded stepchildren of the healthcare system, with minimum insurance coverage allocated for those in need of help. I found this to be especially true in the 1980s and 1990s.) Fortunately, my psychiatrist had coupons that permitted me to receive medicine without having to pay for it.

I tried—really tried—to change my distorted thinking and redirect it in more positive, healthier channels. I wrote and wrote and wrote, putting on paper my thoughts and feelings and trying to come up with possible solutions to various problems. Some of my writings were in the form of a journal, while others were writing exercises that I learned from reading Beck and Beck's books on cognitive behavior therapy. Sometimes these activities would help with the sadness—and then another event would occur, plunging me into a fresh state of despondency. At times I thought I would never stop feeling sad or depressed, but fortunately this proved to be false.

I'd always had an intense fear of rejection, a fear that was initially generated by my father and continued with my sons, who were totally disrespectful to me in their adolescent years. My younger son, James, who is now in his mid-thirties, continues with this disrespect. Rejection translated into pain and a feeling of not being needed or cared about. This, in turn, translated into a loss of self-worth and self-confidence. I would often question the meaning of my life, because those who were closest to me caused me the most pain. Unfortunately, I depended on the opinions of others to gauge my integrity as a human being. I didn't love myself or know how to love myself. I had even taken on the rejection of others and personalized it, which wasn't a healthy thing to do. In my therapy group, for instance, one of the women had rejected her brother because he was grossly overweight and had had a mental breakdown earlier in his life. I felt so bad for her brother that I took on his probable feelings of rejection, for I too am overweight and have had several mental breakdowns. My assumption was that if she had rejected her brother, she would reject me too. When I brought this to the attention of my therapy group, the woman immediately assured me that my assumption and internalization of her rejection were completely unfounded.

My anger is activated when I've been cheated, insulted, criticized, offended, taken advantage of, or provoked. While I have expressed anger verbally under certain circumstances when I justifiably felt provoked, in general I'm not an angry person; I tend to be a pacifist who avoids confrontation as much as possible. When people around me get angry, I hate it and feel uncomfortable. My parents expressed so much anger during their frequent verbal and physical fights that it actually traumatized my sister and me. On the other hand, when I got angry as a child—an infrequent occurrence—I was always physically punished. When I would cry, I was told, "I'll give you something you'll really cry about!" You can see why, as a child, I avoided anger at all costs. The threat of being punished resulted in my trying to be the perfect child and doing everything I was asked to do.

As an adult, I occasionally got angry at my husband, especially when I was working, because he expected me to do everything around the house. I would launch periodic protests, but nothing changed. My anger fell on deaf ears, but I would still object—a useless exercise other than getting the frustration off my chest. The inequity in our marriage almost resulted in divorce.

Arthur's attitude was actually a throwback to an earlier generation. His mother did not work until he was in college, and so she was able to be a den mother and do similar things in Arthur's younger days. (I would be remiss if I didn't add that his mother had someone to do her ironing, cleaning, and baking for her.) Meanwhile, his father went out and earned the money. No wonder Arthur thought the way he did! But even though I understood my husband's viewpoint, it struck me as unfair and made me frustrated and angry. I had expected more parity in our marriage.

I would also get angry with my mentally ill son, James, after which I'd fear for my life due to the possibility of retaliation. He'd do whatever he wanted and then rail at me if I said anything to him about a specific unacceptable behavior. It was easy to get angry at James, for just about everything he did or said was irritating. (Some of the things he did that irritated me were leaving crumbs all over the house, as well as dozens of water bottles and partially filled glasses; using our house as a whorehouse, bringing any girl he wanted to have sex with up to his bedroom; talking to me as if I had no feelings; and getting into trouble with the police.) However, I found myself getting even more upset when I got angry with him. Since then I've learned that it was generally James's irrational, psychotic, delusional thinking and behavior that kept me so upset, and I've recently come to realize that he's not in total control of his illness. When he becomes irrational, I simply protect myself by saying good-bye if I am in his presence or by ending our conversation if we're talking on the telephone. I no longer react with the same intensity as I did in the past; I control my anger by establishing boundaries, setting limits, and taking care of myself. I've realized I'll never be able to convince him of the flaws in his thinking, but life has become much better for both of us since I implemented these restrictions, although now there is limited communication between us.

As I've noted earlier, neither of my sons respected me when they were children. My older son recently confessed that he used to do whatever he wanted as long as he got to play hockey. Since practice and games were important (an idea my husband supported), there was little I could do to coax Edward into behaving. Regardless of what I said, he would flip me off and do whatever else he pleased. Again, my anger fell on deaf ears.

My anger was mostly turned inward because of the dismissive and punishing responses I received during my lifetime. Dr. John, a shaman, psychologist, and Buddhist monk, tried to get me to address the origin of this anger so I might love myself more. As a result, I've written a letter to my deceased father asking one rhetorical question after another about why he said and did such hurtful things to me and how reprehensible and inappropriate they were. Since the letter writing was ineffectual, Dr. John suggested that I release my anger either physically (a term he never clarified, but as violence was not part of my makeup, I did not pay attention to this recommendation) or verbally (which for me meant writing about my anger, which was extremely difficult for me). I've virtually eliminated anger from my behavior because of the responses I've received to it in the course of my lifetime. However, I'm working on this task with the help of my therapist. It's Dr. John's opinion that my chronic fatigue is related to years of repressed anger.

Dr. John also wanted me to love and forgive the little girl inside me. This was a confusing idea that led me to wonder what *he* knew that I didn't. First of all, I could not find or identify the little girl inside me. It seemed to me that I was never a little girl, but always an adult. By the age of nine, I had lost the childish sense of fun and was often unhappy. How could I love and forgive a child who had been constantly beaten down? And why did I need to love and forgive her? Was being *me* my fault? Or was it my parents' fault? I had always had a history of blaming myself for anything that went wrong, and Dr. John knew this. I had continually internalized one line of thinking—that it was *my* fault: my fault that I fought back, my fault that I hated my father, my fault that I was stupid, my fault that I physically matured so early in life, and my fault that I didn't know how to play with other kids or have a good imagination. Now I can see that many of those qualities are the result of being born into a dysfunctional family or having learning issues. None of this was my fault, but that was how I psychologically responded to the world in which I found myself. Suddenly I realized that I *did* need to love and forgive that child within me who was abused and who did not know how to get out of toxic situations. Why hate myself *or* the little girl I left behind? She'd never had proper emotional and intellectual nourishment or guidance. I recognized, with Dr. John's help, that I needed to tell that little girl that she had done the best she could under the circumstances. But even today, clearing that hurdle is complex and difficult, and I realize it may take considerable time to love and forgive myself.

A scary thought that I once stated and that was acknowledged by my psychiatrist, Dr. Dave, is that I have enough rage inside me to kill someone. No wonder I try to suppress my anger—I'm scared of losing control! No doubt this anger and rage will need to seep out in bits and pieces, because addressing it head-on doesn't seem to be the right pathway for me. Recently, when I shared with Dr. Dave that I was angry with my son for his general lack of concern for me (for instance, I would like to get an occasional phone call asking how I am), Dr. Dave said, "Congratulations, you are moving from suicide to homicide!" which made me laugh.

My mother was critical of me for most of my adult life. Finally, at the age of forty, I wrote her a note asking her to stop criticizing me whenever I did anything inconsistent with her thinking. I also felt the need to defend my children against her despite their disrespectful behavior, because she was hypercritical of them too. Though they weren't angels when they were young, they were relatively normal, active children. Mom's philosophy was that children should be seen and not heard. Ultimately, I had to ask her to move out of our home because of the disruption she caused between my children and my husband. I believe to this day that mother criticized me so I'd be a better person, but the degree of her criticism was definitely excessive and detrimental to my self-esteem.

The criticism and abuse I received as a child led me to believe that being perfect would allow me to live in safety. However, as I found out the hard way, that wasn't necessarily a healthy conclusion. My perfectionism led to disappointment, which affected my self-esteem and self-worth. I never expected anyone else to be perfect—just myself. I often told my children to simply do their best and I would be happy with their performance. My husband—half joking, half serious—would say, "They crucified the *last* perfect person!" When discussing perfectionism, Dr. Williams often asked me, "Why do you think they put erasers on pencils?" Yet my mother was a perfectionist. She was hypercritical, and as a result, criticism became my Achilles' heel later in life. For instance, if I had an evaluation from my boss and there was one statement of constructive criticism, I would consider my total performance a failure.

In general, I'm a very trusting person other people have abused for their own benefit. For example, I thought I could trust my uncle, which was an error on my part. I also thought I could trust my parents, but they had their own flaws which were detrimental to both my health and my safety. It could be said that I was naive and gullible rather than street-smart. It always amazes me when I meet a person who is untrustworthy. In my efforts to find a partner since the death of my husband, I have used many Internet dating sites. There are many toads out there; I have yet to find my Prince Charming. But I have learned a lot about trust, and what it is to trust my own instincts, because they are usually correct! I am also more suspicious than ever, especially when it comes to sexual abuse. I am still a trusting person until an internal red flag goes up; then I call a halt to potentially harmful situations. I've found that a lot of guys I've met online can't be trusted. Many of them only want a sexual relationship before getting to know me. I don't mean to imply that I'm asexual, but there is more to a relationship!

There were times I was surrounded by hopelessness; I thought my life would never make a turn for the better. It seemed that every time I made a step forward, I ended up taking two steps back, and I thought I'd never get better. To my credit, however, despite my feelings of despair, depression, loneliness, suicidal thinking, anger, and rejection, I never actually attempted suicide. Nor did I ever resort to self-mutilation such as cutting, which is often seen in people who are depressed. Even when I was in the depths of hopelessness, I continued trying to climb out of the hole of depression, grief, and post-traumatic stress disorder. It's been the hope, prayers, and encouragement of others, as well as their faith in me, that has seen me through the deepest waters. No matter how hopeless I felt, I always tried to do what my therapists and doctors prescribed, because I felt they knew more than I did. Every time I went through a particular crisis, I would thank them for their recommendations and interventions. Their response was always the same: "*You* did the work!"

In college I lost my faith in God because I felt so disappointed in my life and my inability to produce the results I tried so hard to achieve. I honestly thought God had abandoned me; now I know differently, for I've found that God is always there for me. He's proven it over and over again by having helpful people available to me—not only when times get tough, but in good times as well. I've been blessed with wonderful friends, relatives, and providers, a fact that is now apparent, although it wasn't when I was going through some periods, especially my college years. I'm now grateful for all those prayers and the helping hands that God has continually provided for me throughout my life. It *has* taken a village to make me the person I am now—someone who trusts God and has learned to trust herself and her thoughts and feelings.

In spite of my perpetual inner turmoil, I have made myself available to people in need, especially as an oncology nurse. Having also been able to help friends during *their* life journeys has proven to me the validity of the scriptural injunction that it's better to give than to receive.

After the deaths of my husband, my mother, the Prices, my friend Lauren, and my college confidante, Chris, I worried about being overcome with loneliness. I was certainly overcome with grief for a time and would often cry over the many losses in my life. In addition to these losses, I've also mourned the loss of friendships, the loss of my own memory, and the loss of my son James to schizophrenia. They all contributed to the grief I kept imprisoned within me for years.

Oddly enough, one thing that plunged me into extreme sadness after Arthur died was attending church. Instead of finding solace and comfort there, I cried every Sunday for six months after his death because I missed him so much. I think I had some anger toward God for disrupting my life by taking away my lover and my best friend. I saw God as the instigator of my misery. Intellectually, I know that Arthur was better off no longer suffering from the many illnesses related to his hemochromatosis, but emotionally I felt robbed. On the rare occasions when I am feeling lonely, I still go through periods of sadness, but they don't last very long. I have learned to replace the sadness with constructive activities like working on crafts, writing, and reading, as well as studying to be a counselor, which is my goal.

I still never know when something will trigger an emotional response, but I've learned to deal with life's challenges without resorting to irrational and unhealthy thinking, and ideally my reasoning overcomes my emotions. Of course there's still room for occasional sadness and grief, for that's how it *should* be for a healthy human being with normal feelings.

After Arthur died, I was concerned that I'd never find another partner, and I was obsessed with this notion for years, but now my thinking is clearer and I don't worry about it. During the early stages of this obsession, my therapy group suggested that I get a dog or a cat, which I ultimately did. My Himalayan Persian, Cambridge, keeps me company; however, that doesn't mean that a cat can take the place of a warm and wonderful person.

I also have been able to cultivate some amazing friends, and I no longer feel completely lonely. I'd still like to have a partner, but that is no longer the main focus of my life. I'm happy even though I am alone. I'm quite convinced that the majority of my grief work is over, despite certain situations when I will cry because I miss a particular person. I believe this is normal. My obsessive wish for a partner is gone, although I do keep my eyes open for potential candidates. I need to follow God's plan for me, although I don't know exactly what that plan is. I'm certain that there's a place in the universe for me, and that, with time and patience, I'll learn what it is and how it might change over time.

I believe I began to see myself as a failure as a little girl, when I twice failed to be promoted in school, for I had no idea that I was suffering from dyslexia. Because of my parents' expectations and their reaction to my plight, the idea that I was both stupid *and* a failure caused deeper dents in my already-bruised self-esteem. Fortunately, my later successes restored some of my faith in myself. It's clear to me now that seeing myself as a failure was really an all-or-nothing form of self-judgment. Now I see things as they really are: I no longer feel like a failure, but rather like a person who has been on an up-and-down journey. It's been through this journey, fraught with mistakes, that I've learned not just about my inner self, but also about life and the world around me.

To this day, disputes resulting in physical and verbal fights trigger trauma and fear in me. My husband and I had our disagreements. In fact, once I was so upset that I tried to open the car door and jump out while we were driving home so I could escape the pain of the disagreement. I could have severely injured myself, but I found the fighting more distressing than the possibility of physical harm. Even recently, when my grandson was scheduled to be in a fight (he and one of his cronies had decided to duke it out at a certain time and place) and my son Edward put me in charge of resolving the situation, the feelings of trauma and fear rose up in me instantly. I'm such a pacifist that I can't tolerate fighting—verbal or physical—without being traumatized again. In the case of my grandson, I could see where my fear had its roots. Although the situation upset me for several hours, having two plans of intervention in place ultimately resulted in a sense of calm. (The fight never occurred, because I took my grandson shopping. That was Plan A. Plan B was to have the local police department on speed dial if they decided to go at it.)

I also lived in fear that my peers would think poorly of me if they found out that I had a mental illness. I tried my best to hide my sadness and make it through the tough times, even when I was at work, and most of the time I was successful. I believe that many people live with mental illness in fear of being found out, and so there are many closeted mentally ill people who hide their disorder due to the social stigma. When I was working in radiation oncology, I couldn't hide the effects of my depression, as I was unable to overcome the fatigue and sleeplessness associated with it. Being at work by 7:00 or 7:30 a.m. after working the late shift the night before was very difficult for me. In part this was due to the hour-or-two commute to and from work. Sometimes in the winter, the trains were delayed, especially when it was incredibly cold. But my boss always saw these delays as a lack of planning on my part, and being late for work made me paranoid about getting in trouble. As a result, I told my boss that I had significant sleeping problems. Today I understand why she considered me unreliable in failing to get to work on time. When I had a position with a flexible schedule, this was never a problem. Therefore, wanting to appear dependable, I changed my job and returned to outpatient neuro-oncology, where my hours weren't as rigid.

My mental illness was something I didn't want to admit to; no one feels comfortable talking about mental illness or asking mentally ill people how they feel. PTSD has become a recognized disorder only lately, due to the troops who have returned from the Middle East suffering the effects of war. It should be noted that the general population can also suffer from PTSD due to traumatic events such as sexual assault or serious abuse. I became a member of that group because of the traumatic childhood events with my parents and my uncle, plus the damage I did to myself due to a lack of guidance—or my refusal to accept guidance—as a teenager and young adult.

One of the things that generated my negativity was my inability to remember names, events, directions, words, and even general knowledge—a side effect of my own depressive thinking and the ECT. If it were not for my journals and the friends and family members who remembered certain events and tolerated my memory loss, I would not have been able to reconstruct some of the events mentioned in this history. I didn't lose all my long-term memories, however, for I clearly remember the hell I went through as a child, the disappointments I experienced in college, and the sadness and anxiety I suffered during the balance of my life. The recovery process of recalling past events has taken a lot of time, and there are *still* events I can't remember, so I depend upon others to fill in the gaps. Now that I understand, my memory loss isn't as upsetting to me as it once was. It's my hope that I won't go through any more depressive events or ever have to receive ECT again.

Often I couldn't identify what was pushing my mood down, and this was very frustrating. I could be having a great time, engaged in conversation, when out of the blue my mood would plunge. I had no idea what thoughts could have caused such a significant drop. During those periods of extreme sadness, my energy level usually fell, plummeting so low that it was difficult for me to move. If I was with friends—perhaps at someone's home—it wasn't unusual for me to excuse myself and take a rest. Sometimes when I was despondent, I would simply curl up in a ball on a couch or a bed—a common act for sad or deeply depressed people. Sometimes I would simply cry.

As time went by, I learned through the hospital's partial program and a cognitive behavioral therapy group to distract myself with pleasurable activities like going to a movie, knitting, sewing, or making jewelry. I also found distraction in exercising, listening to music, journaling, shopping ("retail therapy," as my husband called it), or calling a friend. I found it better to be active than to ruminate and stay in bed. Sometimes I would write about my feelings of depression or sadness and try to figure out what was causing my mood. Writing exercises, known as mood monitors or chain analyses—were a real help as I was working through difficult thoughts, feelings, and situations. Some of the things that affected my mood were seeing myself as incapable, making mistakes, feeling criticized, having someone treat me poorly when I thought that I was right, and seeing myself as eternally depressed. The writing exercises helped me identify the driving force of my mood and look at my distorted thinking when I felt sad, hurt, angry, or rejected. However, when my feelings were very intense, it was not unusual for me to have to wait a day or two before I could think clearly enough to do a mood monitor. Sometimes I needed to let my feelings calm down—or even sleep on them—before I could actually sort through the problem.

When I volunteered as an ESL (English as a Second Language) teacher and sang in the church choir, I got back more than I gave, for the ability to give to others often leads to feelings of satisfaction, joy, and self-worth. Although I'm unable to work on a full-time basis because of chronic fatigue syndrome, volunteering has added considerable meaning and pleasure to my life and provided some structure to my day. I learned about volunteering at the partial program, and I'm thankful I was exposed to the concept. One of the things that Dr. Dave told me was that it was good to give to others, but not at my own personal expense. When I volunteered to be costume mistress for my high school plays, for example, I worked far too hard and paid the price psychologically for giving what I didn't have the physical energy to give.

Over the years, the healthier I got, the better I coped with sadness and distracted myself from negative and erroneous thinking. However, it took years of therapy and education before I became adept at dealing with problems. Now that I can see things more clearly, I can resolve problems without reverting to my "go-to point" of sadness, anxiety, depression, or suicidal thoughts. I still experience feelings of sadness, loss, and anger, but they don't last long.

The following pieces of wisdom about dealing with life's difficulties are pearls I learned in partial program. They were written by Dr. Dave H. Rosmarin and Dr. Randy Auerbach, and I have their permission to share them with you.

- Life is a test. Struggles make us stronger. The harder it gets, the greater I have to grow.
- We cannot control the outcome, but we can control the process.
- My task is not to solve my problems, but it is best to get through them without making them worse.
- Life changes from day to day. I can improve moment by moment.
- My difficulties are a gift; they are an opportunity for my faith to grow.
- Even when life is difficult, it never ceases to have meaning. (Victor Frankl would agree with this statement. Read *Man's Search for Meaning*.)
- Nothing is permanent, including our thoughts—these change over time.

Recently, at the age of sixty-two, I apologized to my sister for getting angry at her and hitting her because she didn't help out around the house when we were youngsters. Once I had the opportunity to watch other children and see what they are like at the ages of nine and seven, I realized that my mother's expectations for Rae and me were unrealistic. Rae replied that no apology was necessary, that our mother's expectations were indeed unrealistic, and that she had somehow intuitively understood that her job was to play—and that's what she did. Although I agreed with Rae about our mother's expectations, even for a nine-year-old, I had risen to the occasion because it was *expected* of me. To my way of thinking, there wasn't much choice—I could either do what was expected of me or be in trouble. I certainly didn't want to get yelled at, punished, or spanked because I fell down on the job!

The following quote is from the cognitive behavioral therapy class Dr. Lorraine Corso conducted a couple of years ago at McLean Hospital in Belmont, Massachusetts: "Nothing bad can happen to me while I am trying to remain calm."

A friend of mine, Catherine Coleman, was speaking to me about how difficult her previous Christmas had been when she eloquently stated, "We need to give honor to the pain and go on."

When I consulted with Sister Catherine from the Jesuit Center in Watertown, Massachusetts after my recovery from my mental illness diagnoses, she asked me what spoke to me, asked me what spoke to me from my favorite scripture reading, I Corinthians 13. I said what struck me most was Paul's observance that "love never fails," for I've found this to be true in so many situations—regarding not only the love of others, but also the love of self.

There's also the Serenity Prayer, which I believe leads to balance and wisdom:

> God grant me the serenity to accept the things I cannot
> change: Courage to change the things I can; and the

wisdom to know the difference, living one day at a time, enjoying one moment at a time; accepting hardships as the pathway to peace; taking, as He did, this sinful world as it is, not as I would have it; trusting that He will make all things right if I surrender to His Will; that I may be happy in making all things right if I surrender to His Will; that I may be happy in this life and supremely happy with Him forever in the next. Amen

The Prayer of Saint Francis is also something I've tried to live by, despite the many times I've needed help:

Lord,
Make me an instrument of Your peace;
Where there is hatred, let me sow love
Where there is injury; pardon
Where there is doubt; faith
Where there is despair; hope
When there is darkness; light
Where there is sadness; joy
Divine Master grant that I may seek
Not so much to be consoled as to console
Not to be understood; but to understand;
Not to be loved as to love;
For it is in giving that we receive;
It is in pardoning that we are pardoned;
And it is in dying we are born to eternal life.

Amen

Chapter 10

Death at an Early Age

*M*y husband, Arthur, had a long history of medical problems: diabetes, hypertension, cellulitis, the amputation of his left lower leg, obesity, liver failure, hepatocellular carcinoma, thrombocytopenia (a very low platelet count), and esophageal varices. All these problems but the hypertension were ultimately linked to hemochromatosis, a disease in which the body is unable to rid itself of iron. The iron builds up and ultimately affects all the organs in the body, including the largest one, the skin. Besides being bronze from the accumulation of iron, Arthur's skin was very thin and fragile and would tear and bleed easily because of the low platelet counts. Having diabetes exacerbated his many bouts of cellulitis, especially if he bumped into something with his fragile, thin-skinned legs. When the skin on his legs developed an infection, he required frequent and prolonged use of very strong antibiotics, such as vancomycin, administered by IV either in the hospital or at home. Due to the buildup of iron in his pancreas, he developed adult-onset diabetes at the relatively young age of twenty-nine. (He was already a perfect candidate for the disease because it ran in his mother's family and he was significantly overweight.) Diabetics must take special care of their feet, for it's common for people afflicted with the disease to lose toes, feet, or even legs. Arthur developed a wound infection in his left foot from a blister, which subsequently resulted in osteomyelitis (a bone infection). Despite the IV antibiotics and excellent care by both the wound team and the visiting nurses, it was necessary to amputate his left leg below the knee when he was about fifty-five. After the amputation he required rehabilitation and a prosthesis. He also had to walk with a cane for the rest of his life, because the combination of his weight and the prosthesis impaired his balance.

Due to his diabetes (which he essentially ignored for more than twenty-five years, with the exception of taking his medication regularly), he had to void frequently at night, often filling his four urinals between sundown and dawn. I had to empty these urinals frequently so they could be refilled. He also suffered severe leg cramps during the night, for which we tried a number of antidotes—quinine water, moist heat, warm wet towels wrapped in blue pads, and massage. These unpredictable cramps, largely caused by dehydration, were very disturbing and painful for Arthur and problematic for me because very little worked to resolve them. Part of the problem was that he had suffered liver failure that caused an accumulation of large amounts of fluid in the abdomen. As a result he was on restricted fluids and heavy doses of diuretics, which likely caused or exacerbated the leg cramps.

Platelets—the cells in the blood that prevent bleeding—have a normal count of 150,000 to 300,000; Arthur's platelet count was around 19,000, which meant he bled and bruised easily. The low count was a result of Arthur's hemochromatosis, which greatly enlarged his spleen, which in turn destroyed the platelets manufactured by his bone marrow.

Arthur also had esophageal varices, a result of liver engorgement, which put pressure on the blood vessels enervating the esophagus and made them hemorrhage. He would vomit large quantities of blood, which was frightening for all of us, and he occasionally required multiple blood transfusions—a delicate situation, since the blood added volume to his system.

In light of all these symptoms, one of Arthur's work colleagues suggested that he might have hemochromatosis and gave him literature about the disease. What caused her to suspect this was that Arthur's knuckles had enlarged and his skin was changing to a bronze color. Up till then, no one, not even his doctors, could attach a diagnosis to the variety of symptoms that Arthur exhibited. When he was in the hospital for his amputation, he mentioned his colleague's theory to his doctor, who then ordered a genetic test. The results were positive for hemochromatosis, indicating that this inherited disorder was the culprit behind almost all of Arthur's health problems.

In 2003, after Arthur had finished rehabilitation for the amputation, a full workup revealed that he actually had end-stage hemochromatosis, with the involvement of the liver clinching the diagnosis. He was sent to a gastroenterologist and liver specialist who was extremely compassionate, knowledgeable, and honest about what to expect. A CAT scan of the liver revealed multiple lesions. These were presumed to be cancerous, so Arthur had three separate sessions of focal radiation therapy to these lesions. The option of a liver transplant was offered but not genuinely recommended, because the hemochromatosis had already affected most of his organ systems by the time of diagnosis. As a consequence, he was given three to five years to live.

One of the complications of liver involvement is the inability to process ammonia, a by-product of live metabolism. When this happens, ammonia levels build up and the patient becomes very confused. To prevent this complication, Arthur was prescribed lactulose, a viscous liquid that causes the patient to have multiple bowel movements, thus lowering the ammonia levels. Unfortunately, Arthur didn't recognize when he was confused and would argue with me. I'd try to be as gentle and understanding as possible, but issues would come up that required my intervention. For example, Arthur had an incredible sense of direction, but when his ammonia levels were elevated, he would insist that I drive south when I needed to drive north. While driving the car himself, he would often stop at *green* lights. Although he worked with numbers every day of his life and had been an excellent painting estimator, he was unable to calculate the tip when we went out to dinner.

However, Arthur was very brave and rarely complained, except when I was at work and our son James provided care (for which he insisted on being paid four hundred dollars a week). On those occasions, Arthur would cry each night when I arrived home. A very private person, he resisted outside help, even though I believed this was the best option. I wanted to hire a home health aide or an LPN to take care of him during the day, but he objected to the idea, which upset me and made me feel guilty. He hated the care James provided, yet he refused professional care, preferring that *I* take care of him. However, I needed to continue working in order to pay the bills and keep our health insurance. Even though I could take family leave, I didn't have the required three months of earned time (a mixture of sick time, vacation time, and holiday time). Leave would have been granted if I had requested it, but family leave is generally granted without pay. We hadn't saved enough money for me to take that much time off and continue to live without debt, and our insurance would not pay a daily fee in case of illness. We never could have obtained that type of insurance, for Arthur had always been such a poor risk.

Arthur kept the severity of his illness from his colleagues and friends, but when he was advised of his diagnosis, he called all his cousins and warned them that he had a genetic illness and urged them to be tested for hemochromatosis. Unfortunately, two of his cousins had been diagnosed with the disease already but had not told the rest of the family. If Arthur had *known* about the family history of the disease, he would have been tested and treated for it. (The usual treatment for hemochromatosis is monthly phlebotomy, which is usually effective at keeping the disease at abeyance.) This doesn't mean that Arthur wouldn't have died from this awful disease, but perhaps he could have lived longer with fewer problems.

Fortunately, Song came home at the end of the first semester of her senior year at Moore College and stayed until the beginning of her next semester, giving Arthur the excellent, loving care and attention he needed. This made him comfortable, happy, and content. On her first day home, she got her father squared away, put up the Christmas tree, decorated the house, and prepared dinner. She was amazing, and I was extremely grateful. Arthur was happy with his daytime care, and she helped me out of a difficult situation, for I was already taking care of him during the evening, nights, and weekends after working all day.

Eventually Arthur's condition worsened, and he developed another blister on his right heel from rubbing his foot on the sheets to boost himself up in bed. Although he had been given a soft-heel boot, it came a little too late. The blister got infected, and nothing we did—dressing changes, antibiotics, etc.—healed it. This was the beginning of the end. He was hospitalized for IV antibiotics the day after the Super Bowl in 2006, and then he continued treatment in a rehabilitation hospital in the North End of Boston. While Arthur was home, I always provided him with flowers and a scented candle, which he liked. Before he went to the rehab center, I sent him a lovely Valentine's Day bouquet from one of Boston's premier florists. Upon his discharge from the hospital, I asked James to bring the flowers with him to the rehab center. As usual, James didn't listen to my request, and the expensive and beautiful flowers were trashed. I was upset with James's lack of cooperation; however, given all that was happening, it really didn't make any difference. Arthur's blister turned into another osteomyelitis. His liver was decompensating more and more, and he was getting sicker and sicker, regardless of the lactulose and the many uncontrolled bowel movements, which caused him considerable embarrassment.

While Arthur was in rehab, we celebrated his fifty-ninth birthday with a party on March 9. I assembled the kids the day before his birthday, and one of Song's girlfriends, Christine, came over to take a family picture that included the three children; our grandson, Nathan; our cat, Cuddles; our dachshund, Nubbs; and me. We had the picture enlarged and framed for Arthur's birthday present. I also asked the nursing staff to get Arthur dressed the day of his birthday so we could take some final family pictures. I took the day off from work, cooked his favorite Italian foods, and brought everything to the rehab center. We were permitted to use an empty room, where we had a wonderful birthday party and got some memorable pictures. Arthur loved our birthday present; we later placed it in his room, where he could always see his family. When he died, we placed the picture in his casket.

I was with Arthur every weekend and every evening after work while he was in the North End. Allowed to stay as late as I wished, I watched him decline in front of my eyes. On Thursday, March 23, the doctor in charge of Arthur's case met with us at my request. I thought that Arthur needed hospice care. Having been a hospice nurse and having worked largely with oncology patients, I had a sixth sense about when a patient was near death. The doctor replied that Arthur might live another three months and that I needed to fill out Medicaid forms so there would be coverage for his care at the rehab center. I appreciated the doctor's concern regarding payment for the center's services, but I felt his comments were inappropriate and insensitive. However, he *did* speak to Arthur about the possibility of receiving morphine, pointing out the fact that since his filtering system (the liver) was essentially not working, the morphine would accumulate in his body, resulting in a fatal drug overdose. Arthur clearly understood this and consented to the use of morphine, fully aware of the consequences of the buildup of the drug. In fact he was grateful for the suggestion, for he was in terrible pain. He would cry and say, "These mitts don't work anymore," referring to his hands, which were virtually useless to him and caused him intense pain whenever he attempted the simplest of tasks. He could do nothing manually, including feeding himself. The doctor's suggestion that Arthur was suffering from depression left me quite angry. Arthur was never depressed in his life other than when James was taking care of him and when he realized he was dying. I was angry that the doctor hadn't acknowledged Arthur's terminal state. I knew there was no way he could live much longer.

The next day, a Friday, I was extremely restless at work. I knew my husband was going to die soon, and I wanted to be with him when it happened, so I packed up my papers and left for the rehab center. There I sat and held Arthur's hand until he fell asleep, and then I attended to my hospital paperwork. That night I stayed at Arthur's bedside, having asked Edward to come in on Saturday morning so I could go home and shower. Fortunately, he was accommodating. I also asked James if I could temporarily have my computer back, as I wanted to write Arthur's eulogy. Unfortunately, he allowed me to have it for only two days; he seemed oblivious to my needs and cared only about his video games. When he made his next trip to the rehab center, it was to pick up the computer rather than to see his father.

On Saturday, I asked the nursing staff to call in a priest for the Anointing of the Sick. The priest prayed with us and gave Arthur the last rites. I stayed overnight, and on Sunday morning a psychiatric nurse practitioner came in to see Arthur, which surprised me. I told her that I thought Arthur was dying and needed to be in hospice—an assessment she instantly confirmed. I then asked her to call my boss to let him know I would not be coming to work because Arthur was near death. Unfortunately my boss was already dissatisfied with me because I had taken two weeks off earlier in November to sort out Arthur's situation. (Though he was a neuro-oncologist, he exhibited little to no empathy when I was dealing my husband's terrible illness and imminent death. Actually, I had thought a practicing oncologist would totally understand my need to have some time off.)

On Monday morning, Arthur was moved to a hospice room where I remained alone with him, since the rest of my extended family and all of Arthur's family and friends lived in the distant Philadelphia area. Edward came in to visit, of course, and James came by to pick up his computer. Song had already returned to college after Arthur's birthday, as she needed to complete her senior year as a fashion and textile major. Therefore, with only me by his side, Arthur died quietly and peacefully at 10:35 a.m. on Wednesday, March 29, 2006, at the young age of fifty-nine.

Arthur's death was one of a series of significant losses for me, which ultimately resulted in a diagnosis of complicated grief. On December 2, 2002, my good friend and college roommate, Dr. Patricia Schaefer, died when her car skidded on black ice. She was only fifty-one. One of my best friends, Lauren, who had taken care of me when I received outpatient ECT, died April 30, 2005, from complications of multiple sclerosis and chronic lung disease. Lawrence "Dad" Price died on August 3, 2007, from metastatic prostate cancer. My mother, Marie, died March 20, 2008, at the age of ninety-one, due to congestive heart failure and pneumonia. And Glenda "Mom" Price died of Alzheimer's disease and colon cancer on April 10, 2012, at age eighty-four. Unlike my father's passing, each of these deaths had a profound effect on my mood.

To this day I miss my husband very much and wish he was here. My dream of growing old together was not in God's plan, but we have no control over some things in life. Knowing that all those loved ones who died possessed unshakable faith in God is very comforting.

We had two viewings for Arthur—one in Massachusetts and the other in New Jersey—that many people attended. Besides many flowers, Mass cards, and sincere wishes, donations were made to the Oblates of St. Francis DeSales retirement fund. Of the many beautiful poems we received, the following one is my favorite. This poem is copyrighted, and so it too needs to be modified in order to be printed here. For the full intention of the poem, you can find it online.

To Those I Love and to Those Who Love Me
By
Mary Alice Ramisht

When I am gone, release me, let me go;
I have so many things to see and do.
You mustn't tie yourself to me with tears;
Be happy that we have had so many years.
The author speaks about the love they shared over
the years and the tears the one left
behind will probably have. She continues to
state that they will be apart for only a short while,
and that during this time the loved one should
remember the fond memories they had together.
The author continues to say that the departed
will always be near, even though he or she is untouchable.
And if you listen with your heart you will hear
All my love around you, soft and clear.
And then when you must come this way alone
I'll greet you with a smiling "Welcome Home!"

The church where we had Arthur's funeral Mass, St. Charles Borromeo in Cinnaminson, New Jersey, had a liaison, a helpful soul, to aid us through the process of organizing the service. She also baked a large batch of homemade scones and gave us a beautiful picture of Jesus welcoming home a departed soul. This picture, which I find so very comforting, remains in my heart today. Arthur's good friend Father Crossin said the funeral Mass, in which many of my husband's cousins and other family members participated and I offered the eulogy. Both spiritually and musically, it was a beautiful service; even today, I cry when I think about it.

Arthur was buried in Lakeview Cemetery, where my friend Lauren had been laid to rest the previous year. He rests under a large tree on a hill in section 33, for that was his favorite number and there happened to be a plot available there. A marker with a nautical scene rests upon his burial site.

Understandably, the first Christmas without Arthur was difficult. However, the wife of my coworker, Mr. Glenn, dropped off a Christmas ornament accompanied by the following poem. Like the other two poems, this too is copyrighted, and so I've used only eight lines of it. You can read the entire poem online.

Merry Christmas from Heaven
By
John Mooney

I still hear the songs, I still see the lights,
I still feel your love on cold wintry nights …

I still share your hopes and all of your cares …
I'll even remind you to please say your prayers …

*The author continues, stating that the one
left behind makes the deceased proud of
how he or she is managing life. The
deceased encourages the survivor to continue the
climb, even if he or she slips and falls, for
God will forgive these mistakes in difficult times.*

To my family and friends, please be thankful today …
I'm still close behind you in a new special way …

I love you all dearly; now don't shed a tear
'Cause I'm spending my Christmas with Jesus this year …

Arthur is gone but not forgotten. I believe he visits when seagulls are flying around, since he seemed most at home near a body of water. He loved to sail, fish, and go tubing down the Delaware River from Point Pleasant, Pennsylvania. I am convinced that even on a desert he would have been able to find a puddle somewhere, due to his incredible optimism and passion for water (not to mention the fact that he was a Pisces). He has come to me three times in dreams over the nine years I've been a widow. I miss him terribly, but it was neither my fault nor my *choice* that he died at such an early age.

Peace, dear—peace.

Chapter 11

The Challenges of
Being a Widow

$\mathcal{L}$ife changes radically as soon as you become a widow. There are many aspects that change, from being alone and doing things by yourself to knowing you have the capacity and responsibility to do what you want without needing to consult your partner. Following the death and burial of my husband, the first decision I needed to make was when to return to work. The social worker in our department suggested that I take a couple of weeks off, since I had earned enough time to do so—this was in addition to the three days of bereavement granted by the hospital when a spouse dies. However I returned the Monday after Arthur's funeral, crying every day for the next six months as I drove to the hospital, because of the amount of work that needed my attention. I was used to riding to work with Arthur occasionally during the time we lived in Massachusetts, except during his final years, when he became so disabled that he could only work from home. For the first six months after his death, my mind tended to drift while I was driving, and as a result I had a couple of accidents. I didn't realize that my concentration had been disrupted by incredible sadness and loneliness.

Six weeks after Arthur died, I began attending grief group meetings held at my church under the direction of our parish nurse, Nan, who is warm, sensitive, compassionate, understanding, and loving. They were very helpful, for I was able to summarize in my grief journal many of the events associated with Arthur's life and death. It was through this group that I received the following guidelines for taking care of yourself during the grief process. I've modified them to be consistent with my own experiences.

- Realize and accept that the process of grief will take time. Everyone grieves at a different rate.
- Realize and accept that in a state of grief you are not up to doing what you used to do, and that some things will take longer and others will just not get done.
- Realize and accept that things are different now and you will cope better some days than others.
- Be proud of yourself for the little successes you accomplish.
- Realize and accept that some days you will behave well and other days you'll act crazy.
- Give yourself time to grieve and ruminate, but put a limit on the amount of time you spend doing so.
- Find something you enjoy doing, and do it every day. It is important to find pleasure in life while grieving.
- Especially during the first year, limit the number and complexity of things you need to decide on or change.
- You may feel so emotional that you make decisions with your heart and not your mind.
- Do something you have to do every day, such as pay bills, do laundry, tend to the car, etc.
- Most important, remember to take care of yourself: eat right, exercise, remember to take medications that you have to take, and keep your doctor appointments.

- People will want to help you but won't know how or what to do. Give them suggestions so that you get the help you need. Remember, not everyone will respond to you the way you expect them to.
- Move gently through your emotions toward the one you lost. Keep his or her true nature in perspective; everyone has faults and virtues.
- Remember to stay in touch with your family and friends. Reach out to someone every day. It is important not to isolate yourself.

Despite my grief, I did find that it was becoming easier to concentrate on my job, for I no longer had to worry about an extremely ill husband; that portion of my life was over. Meanwhile, although I thought I was performing my hospital duties in a responsible manner, one of the nurse practitioners in my department continued to ask me on a regularly basis how I was doing. I sensed her genuine interest—and became increasingly aware that I *wasn't* doing well. In fact, I began to recognize that I was becoming more depressed. I wasn't surprised. In addition to James's continued issues, my mother had come to stay with me for several months for moral support. Her presence was a blessing and a curse, for though she was very supportive of me, she saw the stress and strain James was causing around the house, and she had great difficulty tolerating his self-centered behavior and irrational, cutting comments. I too was having significant issues with him on a daily basis. His unacceptable behavior had actually gotten worse after Arthur's death. He became more domineering and controlling as the days passed. It was as if he were the man of the house, at least he thought and acted that way. Since I was the center of his delusional system, he tended to direct all his anger toward me, making no effort to gain insight into his own condition. Perhaps that was beyond his mental capacity. He felt entitled to everything the world offered, because he was a twenty-five-year-old white American male. He couldn't get along with anyone for a sustained period of time, and thus he became isolated. (The exceptions were his Internet buddies, with whom he would play war games into the wee hours.) Anyone who actually spent time around James would have had issues with his outrageous, demanding, disrespectful, psychotic behavior.

By the end of April, it became apparent that I needed to make some changes in the household. Convinced it would be best for my mother, I took her back to my sister's South Hampton home, thus relieving some of the tension caused by rifts between Mom and James. By June, however, I was receiving calls from my mother complaining that no one would take her food shopping, despite the fact that there were four drivers in the house—my sister, brother-n-law, niece, and nephew—who should have been able to meet her needs. From my distant perspective, my mother, who was ninety years old and no longer driving because of her age and severe arthritis, was an undemanding person with simple needs: food shopping, periodic doctor appointments, and prescription pickups. She also appreciated having company, for she was lonely most of the time. Unsure of what to do, since she lived in Pennsylvania and I lived in Massachusetts, I called my brother-in-law Bryan and asked if he would take her food shopping. Bryan had always loved my mother, whom he referred to as Mrs. M., and he willingly offered to be of assistance, continuing the service for the entire summer. However, I could tell that my mother was unhappy and needed more attention. She bitterly complained about how my sister would not join her for a cup of tea every once in a while. (It should be noted that Rae was working full-time herself.) In an effort to solve the grocery problem, I called all the supermarkets in the area, but none of them had delivery service. I then suggested that my mother take a cab to the store (since she liked hanging on to the shopping cart and selecting her own food), after which she could pay the cabby a few extra dollars to carry the groceries into the house for her. However, this was not an acceptable alternative to my ninety-year-old mother, who simply expected her family to take care of her basic needs.

By October I had heard enough complaining. My mother was genuinely unhappy, but she did not know how to ask for help (a problem I also had). She often admitted that she felt like "a rat in a hole"—especially since her apartment was in the basement of my sister's home. Very little natural light came through its high, garden-level windows except for in her bedroom and bathroom. Finally, frustrated by my mother's complaints yet feeling sorry for her, I drove down to Philadelphia, planning to bring her back with me to Massachusetts in an attempt to make life happier for her. Though I have no recollection of speaking to my sister or brother-in-law about this plan, I am sure I must have discussed it with them. I'm equally sure my sister felt a sense of relief, for my mother had lived with her for many years, and it had been six years since my mother stopped driving a car.

I'm not sure what I was thinking, since James and Edward were still living at home. It never occurred to me that the same scenarios would play out as before, since the same cast of characters was in place. Still, as I was under the combined stress of grieving for my husband, working full-time, and having the two boys living at home, thinking clearly was not one of my strengths. I was shooting from the hip in an effort to resolve everyone's issues except *mine*, unaware of how many issues of my own I had at that time. Once again I put aside my personal needs and issues and focused on making my mother happy, or at least trying to. I think this temporarily postponed the grieving process necessary for me to deal with the deaths of my husband and friends.

Knowing that having adequate nutrition was one of Mom's essential needs, I had the refrigerator stocked with all types of food, including several healthy microwavable items. There were salad fixings, vegetables, fruits, and some luncheon meats, in addition to plenty of snacks that would be easy to grab and eat. Upon returning from work at about 7:00 on that first Monday night, I asked Mom what she'd had for dinner, to which she replied, "A bologna sandwich." For three consecutive nights, I got the same answer to the same question. It didn't take me long to realize that the woman who had helped me out five month earlier now needed more help herself. Since I worked late into the evening at the hospital and had a two-hour journey home, I knew that, realistically, I could care for my mother adequately only on weekends, and so I quickly made arrangements with Meals-on-Wheels to deliver a decent dinner each evening. Unfortunately, though the balanced meals were delivered promptly, she didn't like the food. Taking care of my mother was not going to be an easy, quick fix.

I also called Elder Services to get in-home assistance, since I could properly cook for and bathe Mom only on weekends. Elder Services provided two caregivers: one in the morning who washed and dressed her and gave her lunch, and one in the afternoon to make certain that she ate dinner. Admittedly, this was an excellent, low-cost solution. Mom was much happier knowing there were people in the house who cared about her. On weekends I took over Mom's care—cooking for her, bathing her, and taking care of her toenails and fingernails, as well as taking her out on little jaunts or shopping trips. I had secured a transport chair for her (something like a wheelchair without the large side wheels), and it was a great help in getting her around. Knowing my mother was a devout Catholic, I asked Nan, the parish nurse from our church in Franklin, to come by and give her Holy Communion. Nan was already a welcome tradition in our household; she had been there earlier for Arthur. I also knew Nan as the spiritual leader of the bereavement group I attended shortly after Arthur died. She is an amazing person, and Mom genuinely loved her visits.

One of the things my mother never shared with me was how much money she had—information I needed to make reasonable decisions about her care, because I personally did not have the financial resources to take care of her. She had always kept this information close to the vest. I was privy to the fact that she had a couple of certificates, and that Rae and I were named as beneficiaries in the event of her death. However, I never had any idea how much money Mom had in her possession, although I knew her goal had always been to leave money to Rae and me. My personal belief, which I shared with Mom many times, was that the money was there for her use and care. So I sat down with her and talked about her resources. We decided that I should be her power of attorney. However, I was flying by the seat of my pants in this regard, having never been in this legal position before. I went online and found a model document for power of attorney in Massachusetts, the use of which—as a prototype—cost about twenty-eight dollars. Once I formatted it with my mother's information, we had it notarized and then shared the information with those who needed to know. The agreement was that I was to handle her financial affairs and meet all her personal needs with the help of other providers, since it was impossible for me to take care of her by myself. Although she had always taken excellent care of her money and checkbook, she no longer needed to worry about handling her personal finances. She was grateful to be able to hand this responsibility over to me, for she no longer wanted to make any crucial decisions. I, in turn, was more than happy to help her out; she had been there for me so many times that I wanted to be there for her when she needed me most. I felt that by taking on this responsibility and giving Mom the love and care she so needed, I would have no regrets later. This proved to be true.

One of the first things we did was decide on Mom's health insurance, because her Pennsylvania insurance would not cover her in Massachusetts. This decision was quickly squared away based on Mom's medical issues and needs. I connected with her primary-care physician, took her to her doctor appointments, and made sure she had the medicine she needed.

I hadn't expected to fall into the role of caregiver within several months of Arthur's death. It's interesting to see how divinely managed everything was, for had he been alive (and even in good health), I wouldn't have been able to take care of my mother. Arthur was no fan of hers, largely because she spoke her mind and was critical of how he managed things. In retrospect and in all honesty, Mom was correct 99 percent of the time. When they *both* were alive, I became the sounding board for each of them. Mom saw Arthur as lazy and unhelpful— largely because he was very sick, especially during the last year of his life.

One December morning, just as I was getting ready to walk out the door to go to work, I realized that my mother was in congestive heart failure. She was very weak and fatigued and was having difficulty breathing because of the fluid in her lungs. I immediately called for an ambulance, which took her to a regional hospital, where she was admitted with diagnoses of congestive heart failure, respiratory failure and a respiratory infection. Whenever she was febrile, she would become delirious, and in her delirium, she would feel like she was falling. During the time that I spent with her, I would comfort her and reassure her that she was not falling. I continued going back and forth from my own work in the daytime to the hospital every evening, and I spent my entire weekends with her.

After being released from the hospital, Mom spent some time in a nursing facility in Milford. I remember trying to make Christmas for her with a tree and some decorations. My sister came up to visit her from Philadelphia and gave her a Go-Phone. Rae had hoped that Mom would be able to call her family and friends, but the phone proved impossible for our mother to use. Soon afterward, Mom returned home and we resumed elder services along with my interventions. But as time went by, I realized she needed more assistance than all of us together could provide for her. Around the start of May 2007, I could see that she was slowly going downhill, though she never complained. It became necessary for me to get my mother additional care, so I started visiting nursing homes and assisted-living facilities. Even as a nurse, I wasn't sure what type of facility was best for her. Trying to make the best decision possible, I opted for an assisted-living facility in my community. It cost more than $4,000 a month—a price that included only fifteen minutes of individual care per day, maximum! Obviously, my mother needed more care than that, so I contracted for additional services. However, I didn't opt for pharmacy services, which would have been an additional expense, because I knew *I* could take care of her medications.

Mom moved into the assisted living facility in June 2007. The day after she moved in, the temperature was ninety-four degrees, and to make matters worse, the air-conditioner in her room was broken. Being ninety-one years old, she couldn't tolerate the heat. That night when I arrived there after work, her room was *bloody* hot, and she was nearly stroking out due to the heat. I instantly put cold compresses on her and brought in a fan from home, feeling very unhappy with the way the facility was dealing with the situation. That evening, I told the nurse on duty that I expected the air-conditioning unit in Mom's room to be either repaired or replaced by the time I returned the following day. Fortunately the next day was cooler, and the air conditioner had been repaired and never broke again. Things had gotten off to a shaky start, but they greatly improved from that time forward.

I often got angry at James. One night on the drive home from work, I received a phone call from him, saying he had called Rae and told her that I had put our mother in a nursing home! On the surface, this might have seemed an innocent act on his part. However, since I'd made all the arrangements for Mom's care myself, I had wanted to speak with Rae and fill her in on the details after I had everything sorted out. My sister had attended to many of Mom's needs over the years while Mom lived with her; I felt it was my turn to do the same. Rae was working full-time at a very demanding job, and my goal had been to wait until I could present a completed plan to her. When James took it upon himself to share my plans with her, I went ballistic, especially since he had never helped Mom in any fashion during the years that they lived in the same house. I was so upset that I couldn't stop screaming, probably because of all the stress I had been under trying to arrange for Mom's care while working full-time and doing everything in and around the house as well. That included picking up after my pig of a son, grieving the loss of my husband, and attempting to deal with my own significant depression. I shook and cried all the way home after that phone call from James, wondering how he could have acted with such arrogance.

My mother initially felt that I had dumped her at the assisted-living facility in order to get rid of her, even though I assured her that was not the case. She was actually started on a mild antidepressant, which I think she could have used all her life, and this and the passage of time helped tremendously in her adjustment to her new surroundings. In October 2007, while on one of our weekend trips to Panera Bread, she reached over and took me by the arm and said, "This was the best thing you could have done for me." Even though it had taken several months for her to adjust, which is natural for older people, I was thankful to know she was at last happy.

I visited her at least five times a week. I took her out to have her hair and nails done, drove her to many doctor appointments, got all her prescriptions, arranged for her medications, did all her laundry, paid her bills, took her on outings, and increased the services she received as time went by. Despite the many services required to meet her needs, things were easier and safer for Mom in her new setting, rather than under the old arrangements of living with me and having service providers come into my home while I was at work. Furthermore, she made friends with several people at the facility and was looked upon as a nice and kind person—something that had not happened very often earlier in her life. She even made friends with her male next-door neighbor, who sat at her table in the large and lovely dining room where the residents ate their meals. As a result of her little kindnesses, such as helping him open the coffee creamers, he became attached to her and even wanted to take her to the Cape on a family outing. Because of this gentleman's attention to her, I began to see, for the first time in my life, a little twinkle in my mother's eye.

Unfortunately, she developed another episode of congestive heart failure shortly thereafter and had to be hospitalized. Subsequently she was placed in a nursing home, where she would stay for her remaining days. The head nurse there would always kindly inform me when my mother needed to make a hospital visit.

On the weekend before my mother died, she was very alert. She hadn't been eating much, and I could tell that she was nearing the end of her life. Fortunately my cousin Mike had come to visit from Indiana, and the three of us had a great time talking and laughing about various events that had happened during our lives. We also discussed our plans for the future, including his plans to adopt another child and take a family trip to Disney World. That Saturday, before leaving the nursing home, I asked Mom if she wanted anything special to eat; I felt that she was nearing the end. She said she wanted *sopressata* (an Italian salami) on an Italian roll, chips, and a Coke. Having never heard of sopressata, I asked my dear widow friend, Irene, where I could find an Italian deli, and she directed me to Oliva's Market, where I was able to get the things Mom wanted. Upon arriving at the nursing home with the food, I found Mom once again awake and alert. I didn't care at this point that the sopressata and potato chips contained a lot of salt. That night turned out to be an awesome one, for Mom sat up in bed and ate the entire meal, watching and listening to the Italian tenor Andrea Bocelli on television. She was both peaceful and happy—even joyous—during this wonderful time together. She cracked a joke about Andrea Bocelli, saying, "He always looks like he needs a good scrubbing down." It was a wonderful evening, and the weekend couldn't have been better.

On the following Tuesday evening, while I was at the nursing home, Mom was running a fever and had difficulty breathing. I spoke with the head nurse, and we jointly agreed that Mom needed to go to the hospital. An ambulance was called, and I met my mother at the regional hospital, in the emergency room. X-rays showed she had pneumonia. The ER doctor put her on some oral antibiotics and sent her back to the nursing home, which led to a discussion (more like a disagreement) with the doctor. I was convinced that she needed to be hospitalized, while his philosophy was "that's why they have ambulances." I was quite upset by his orders, knowing that my mother was very sick and needed more care than she could receive at a nursing home.

The following day, while I was driving on the Massachusetts Turnpike, headed from work to the nursing home, the nurse there called to tell me they were sending my mother back to the same hospital that had discharged her the night before. I agreed to meet her there. En route, I called Rae and told her I thought Mom was going to die soon, suggesting it would be best if she came up to Massachusetts from Pennsylvania. She arrived in time to see that our mother was very close to death. My sister lay on the bed and cried and cried, knowing that our mother wasn't going to be with us much longer.

Mom died in the wee hours of Holy Thursday, March 30, 2008. Arrangements were made in Massachusetts for her body to be transported back to Pennsylvania. Rae had recently purchased a beautiful pink nightgown and robe for Mom, and we bought some matching pink slippers for her to wear in the casket. I offered my crystal rosary beads to be buried with her. (Rae wanted to keep our mother's beads, for Mom had faithfully said her rosary every day.) It was Holy Week, and the focus was on Easter, not on funerals, so we waited until Easter Monday to have the wake, which was held at my sister's church in Feasterville, followed by burial at a local cemetery. Unfortunately Rae was quite sick—possibly because she had been so physically close to Mom, lying on the bed next to her as she was dying of pneumonia—and was unable to help plan the funeral Mass. However we talked together, and I made some suggestions for the readings and the songs, which Rae accepted. Meanwhile I was running around like crazy trying to get the program for the service together and make the burial arrangements.

During the Mass, the priest said that people who die during Holy Week go straight to heaven. Whether this is myth or reality didn't matter, because the thought brought comfort to our lives and smiles to our faces. I knew that Mom was already in heaven with Jesus, for she was a good person and was very spiritual.

After interment in the cemetery of my mother's choice (she'd told us she did not want to be buried "on top" of her husband), we hosted a nice reception at a local restaurant. Our cousin Karl gave a wonderfully sincere and humorous eulogy about our Mom. Everyone liked his delivery, and there were both laughter and tears. Karl's mother, Evie, was Mom's sister, and the three of them (Evie, Karl, and Mom) had spent a lot of time together, so Karl knew our mother very well. Following the death of Aunt Evie, Karl would frequently stop by my mother's apartment for a visit and something to eat. It was fitting that he deliver the eulogy and that it be delivered in a restaurant after the funeral, due to its humorous nature.

At Mom's funeral, everyone got along with each other, which sometimes didn't happen at our family's weddings and funerals. I believe we were finally able to come together because the cast of characters had dwindled to the point that those who had harbored strong opinions in opposition to others' were essentially gone. Fortunately, we cousins had knitted together the family breach, for we'd always loved each other and had never lost the closeness we had felt as children. This remains a real blessing; we are able to stay in touch through Facebook and other social media despite being scattered around the country.

As a widow, one of my most difficult ongoing problems has been managing my son James. This challenge isn't unique to me, of course. Many people find it difficult to deal with family members who have severe mental health problems, especially schizophrenia, bipolar disorders, and borderline personality disorders. James's failure to comply with his medication regimens led to the acceleration and exhibition of his psychosis. He refused to listen to me or do anything I asked him to do. It was as if I were invisible. While living at home, he spent most of his time playing video games online rather than working. He lived to play war games on the Internet and had no real friends other than the people who played with him in the evenings and throughout the night. He spent most of his time in his bedroom unless he was in the kitchen preparing a sandwich, a pizza, or Hot Pockets. He would eat these in his bedroom, which was littered with dirty dishes and silverware and at least fifteen empty plastic water bottles. Until recently, we were forever getting into arguments, which upset me and my mother too. After working all day and caring for Mom's needs, I would also have to clean up James's messes. Every day when I got home, I could see where he had been, for he left a messy trail, like Hansel and Gretel. He referred to me daily as "being on crumb patrol." Though I was neat, I was not obsessively so; I merely liked things to be put away after use. This is what led to the clashes between us. Unbelievably, today James is obsessively neat in his own apartment. Who would have thought it?

One of the problems of being the parent, spouse, sibling, or friend of an adult child who has an illness is that you may speak *to* the physician and tell him or her anything you want, but the physician is not allowed to give you any information without the patient's consent. Due to HIPAA regulations, clinicians with a common patient need to have the patient's written permission to talk to each another about him or her. Although I completely understand the merits of the law, it is as if doctors are sworn to secrecy.

When my husband was alive, he would take a backseat when it came to dealing with James's issues. I was the one who needed to communicate with James's treatment team. Because I was in therapy to help me deal with the tremendous stress in my own life, I would usually share my current challenges with my therapist or psychiatrist and we would discuss potential plans. When the water got deep and rough while I was dealing with James, I was always thinking about what I needed to tell his providers. This was especially true when I was riding home from work on the train, since that's when I had a lot of time to think about what I wanted to say. (Sometimes I drove to work and other times I took the Commuter Rail; either way it took about two hours to get to and from there.) After James turned eighteen, however, the only times Arthur and I could communicate with his treatment team were when the social worker requested a family meeting.

Since James can generally keep his behavior under control for fifteen minutes, and since his appointments with the psychopharmacologist/ psychiatrist were generally scheduled only once every few months, I firmly believe that, to this day, his clinicians have no idea how James *really* behaves on a daily basis. (He no longer sees a therapist, he has been dismissed by his case manager from the Massachusetts Department of Mental Health, and he is no longer permitted to participate in the community center for mentally ill patients—I assume because of his obnoxious and disrespectful behavior.) Once James was eighteen, he started "firing" the clinicians who didn't do what he expected them to.

Around the age of twenty-six, James attempted to put into motion the termination of one of the best psychiatrists he ever had, a genuinely compassionate lady who was very thorough, but whose abilities and sincerity James failed to appreciate. Furthermore, he attempted to sue the hospital where she worked for $5 million and also attempted to sue me for $500,000 and have my nursing license revoked. His rationale, and I use that word loosely, was that he was not getting the treatment he thought he deserved and was entitled to. Although he submitted two very long documents that were handled by the courts via the sheriff's department, he failed to identify a plausible complaint. The counsel for the hospital immediately recognized this and quickly put an end to the suit against it. Needless to say, James's action was very upsetting to me, and it cost me several thousand dollars in attorney's fees to do the same thing the hospital counsel did. I was even afraid that James would kill me—a worry I shared with my coworkers. His threatening behaviors and incredible anger toward me not only unnerved me, but also made me sad, distrusting, and fearful.

Often I felt obligated to write letters—*long* letters—to James's psychiatrists and therapists, describing his behavior and noting that stimulants seemed to exacerbate his psychosis. When he was still seeing a therapist, I'd call her and try to fill her in about his behavior and psychotic episodes, but there was rarely any change in his personality, behavior, or thinking. He was (and continues to be) eternally angry at me, blaming *me* for his illness because of the variety of mental illnesses on my side of the family. The only time he verbalizes his love for me is when I give him something. For instance, after he was discharged from a hospital and I forbade him to return home, instead giving him several thousand dollars so he could move to a better, safer location, he told me he loved me and gave me a kiss.

James saw me as part of his delusional system, and I realized this wasn't a good place to be. For a long time, James didn't want to improve his lot; he expected me to cater to his every need and keep him in the lifestyle he had been accustomed to as a child. More recently, he has attempted to work while staying within the financial confines that allow him to quality as disabled. Sometimes he's fortunate enough to find part-time work, while other times there's no work available or he just doesn't want to work. He has a strong sense of entitlement when it comes to money from the government or from me. He sees me as his personal ATM (otherwise known as the Bank of Mom). A few years ago, he started a business selling flags on weekends at open-air flea markets during the spring, summer, and fall. To his credit, he maintained very careful records and managed his business without help most of the time, except for occasional requests for money to restock his flag supply. Recently he told me that his illness doesn't prevent him from finding a job, but that associating with people disturbs him. He is extremely distrustful of others (partly due to his paranoia), he's homophobic, and he also believes there are associations (such as the Mafia) within companies that impede his ability to get a job. Though I don't see James trying to get a job, I can't totally judge him, for I've been unable to work for the past six years due to my own mental illness. However, I *did* work—despite my mental illness—for thirty-three years, with just one interruption when I was first diagnosed.

As part of his psychosis, James has irrational ideas and feelings of great power in the realms of religion and politics. To this day, he believes he has tremendous influence on the "settlement" in the Middle East. He is certain 9/11 wouldn't have happened had he not been hospitalized the previous day. He also believes he is a direct descendant of both Jesus Christ and the British monarchy. Furthermore, he believes that Edward isn't his full brother, and that his paternal grandmother belonged to a different family. Because I'm part Italian, he believes I'm part of the Mafia. Despite the fact that none of these ideas is true, he and I have logged countless hours of discussions, text messages, and rebuttals about his delusional thinking. In the past, I would get really upset and try to reason with him, but now I realize there's no reasoning with a psychotic person. Though I am saddened by James's illness, I've had to set up boundaries and quickly end any discussion of these notions or any others he comes up with. I might make one or two statements, and then I'll say that I can't discuss whatever he's going off about; I tell him that I love him but it's time for me to leave. After I leave, I don't call him; I wait until he calls me, which might be days or even months later.

Before I learned how to deal with James, I made the terrible mistake of driving down to Philadelphia with him in his car; he wanted company, and I wanted to visit some of my family and friends. On the way down, he started to become paranoid, insisting that the people in the cars behind us were Mafia members who were following us all the way down the New Jersey Turnpike—an idea he couldn't let go of. Because the constant barrage of these comments made me extremely anxious, I suggested stopping at the carnival being held at our old church in Cinnaminson, New Jersey. I wanted to see some of our old friends from church, and I knew they would be there, since I had worked the carnival for several years with the same core group of people. When we lived in Central Jersey, James used to go to the carnival every night of the week when it was in town, and so I suggested that maybe he could go on a few rides, get something to eat or drink, and see some of his former buddies. In return he "allowed" me fifteen minutes with my old friends. Unfortunately, when I returned to the car, James was furious, cursing and screaming at me because I had overstayed my allotted time by ten minutes. Being on no time schedule himself, he announced that he was going to meet up with some friends who lived about five minutes away and hang out with them for the remainder of the night. I was so upset by his demeanor that I curtailed my trip, got a hotel room, and took a bus back to Massachusetts the next morning. To exacerbate matters, while walking from the motel to the Mount Laurel bus terminal the next morning, I stepped on a bee and was stung. I'm moderately allergic to bee stings, and so it was as though the bee had added insult to injury.

I've learned not to put myself in those situations with James when there is no escape. If I ride in the car with him now, it's only for a very limited time and distance. Additionally, I conduct any business matters with him in a common area, not within the confines of my condo; this way we both try to keep our cool.

Finally it got to the point where I could no longer deal with my younger son. The next time he was hospitalized because his behavior was off the wall, around 2008 or 2009, I told the social worker that I could not allow him to return home. (It was during that hospitalization that James got physically violent with the staff psychiatrist, and to this day he is no longer allowed in that hospital.) The social worker gave James my message that he had to move out of the house. James was in the hospital for several weeks this time, and upon his discharge, his state case manager gave him one day of assistance finding an apartment and working out the necessary arrangements. Although I was still stressed by James's behavior, I realized that he needed more than one day to find an apartment, gather his things together, and get his finances organized.

Following his discharge, I saw and talked with him regularly, helping him and his intended roommate, Carol, locate an apartment and get settled. Carol's mother helped, gathering such things as a toaster, pots and pans, and other kitchen items. I took James to the Salvation Army, where we picked up a white kitchen table with an inlaid tile top and matching chairs, as well as a brass and glass-topped coffee table. I bought him a bedroom set from a wholesale store so it would be adequate without costing a fortune, and I gave him a set of dishes, a microwave, and many items for the bathroom. I then helped him clean the apartment and did some painting. I asked a friend of mine and her strong son to move James's belongings from his bedroom to the garage, since he was no longer permitted to enter my house, and once that was accomplished, the local police arrived to supervise the move (as ordered by the court), and James arrived with his U-Haul. All this organization made the move go very smoothly.

I mentioned earlier that I always associated my husband with seagulls, since he seemed most at home near any body of water. I reiterate this now due to an unusual occurrence the day of James's move. Wanting to show my appreciation to my friend and her son for helping me move James's things from his room to the garage, I drove to the local Panera Bread to pick up some pastries. When I reached the parking lot, it was as though all the seagulls in town had assembled there. Needless to say, I immediately felt Arthur's presence, and I knew that he approved of my decision not to allow James to continue living in our home. I'll never forget the joy I felt when I saw all those seagulls, and how comforted I was by the feeling of Arthur's presence.

The apartment James shared wasn't well insulated, but the landlord had promised to paint the outside and repair the insulation in the bedroom walls; he did neither. He was a slumlord in every sense of the word. Of course, James had his faults too. For example, he wasn't the cleanest person in the world. After three months, Carol moved out for reasons still unknown to me. Meanwhile James had connected with the local center for people with mental health issues, and I think that actually helped him. He also got a part-time job at a small specialty store, building furniture and stocking shelves. I firmly believe that having a job and making connections with other people helped him. If his father had still been alive, I'm not sure how easily all these changes would have transpired.

Unfortunately, James had become very overweight, and his size proved to be a huge emotional burden for him. He connected with a weight center that charged $1,000 to participate in a program that would qualify him for gastric bypass surgery. I gave him the money, but he backed out of the program. A year later he joined the program again and wanted another $1,000. I refused to pay the second time, since it was obvious that he had misspent the first $1,000. Unable to acknowledge his mistake, he directed his anger toward me for refusing to foot the bill again. Nevertheless, he underwent bariatric surgery and lost a lot of weight very quickly. Prior to his surgery, I asked him if he needed a ride to or from the hospital, if he wanted me to be there during the surgery, or if he would need anything at all postoperatively. He said no to all these questions, since he wasn't too thrilled with me at the time.

When he got home, however, he asked me to bring him a blender to mix the shakes he was supposed to drink. I told him I would bring him one the next day. When I did not show up at the precise time we'd agreed on, he called me. I assured him that I was on my way but had to stop by Edward's home for a few minutes first. This caused him to become extremely angry, and he cursed me out once again. By this time on our journey through life, I was able to tell James that I was not going to bring him the blender, and that I didn't expect to be addressed in that matter, especially when I was doing him a favor. (Though I lived only forty-five minutes from James's apartment, my lack of promptness was difficult for him; any change in plans was hard for him to tolerate.) The need must have been filled, however, for he lost a lot of weight and continued to look very good, although he eventually gained back a fair amount due to a lack of exercise and poor eating habits. On occasion, James still eats salads and vegetables rather than his usual diet of Hot

Pockets, pizza, and ham sandwiches with lots of mayonnaise, plus countless bottles of Gatorade.

James continued to harass me. I've had to file restraining or no-harassment orders against him from time to time over the last fourteen years. Even when Arthur was alive, we had restraining orders taken out on James. Later, without a husband to help me, I had to negotiate this process alone (although I had the emotional support and guidance of my therapists, Dr. Holly and Dr. Dave). In 2011, I took out a no-harassment order because James continued to plague me with constant demands for large sums of money, which as a widow on disability, I couldn't fulfill. This was not the first time he'd demanded large sums of money. When he was in college, he got a job selling Cut-Co Knives, and instead of taking orders and delivering the knives when they were available, he insisted we give him $16,000 so he could stockpile them and have them available at the time of sale. This may have been a good idea, but we did not have the money to invest in such a venture. Cut-Co Knives are excellent but expensive. This was not like stockpiling Girl Scout cookies to sell outside a grocery store or a busy train station.

In 2012, I went before the court and asked for the renewal of the no-harassment order, because James had resumed his previous behavior once the 2011 order expired. The judge denied my request simply because James hadn't violated the previous year's restraining order. I found his decision inconceivable, and it left me horrified and afraid. On the recommendation of Dr. Dave, I hired a lawyer and tried to get a court-appointed guardian for James. I was tired of dealing with his continual demands, especially the financial ones; I no longer wanted to be considered his personal ATM. However, my attempt to obtain a guardianship for James was unsuccessful because the lawyer I had hired was terminating her practice and didn't have time to see the process through to its conclusion. However, she was marginally instrumental in obtaining another restraining order. This time I wrote down a list of the events and issues that had transpired over the years with James, and after the judge read it, he asked, "Why didn't you tell me this the *first* time?" I explained that those details wouldn't have been the proper response to his initial question, which was "Why did you get a no-harassment order on James in 2011?" Now, with my list in hand, the judge ordered that James be escorted from the courtroom immediately. On the way out, James shouted, "You mean you are going to let a murderer free?" Once the court officer was assured that James had left the parking lot, my attorney and I were escorted out of the courthouse.

One of the most difficult things about having a no-harassment or restraining order against my son was that my heart worried about him every day. In spite of James's irrational behavior, I genuinely cared about his welfare, and this perpetual concern eventually led me to the decision, in 2013, to not continue the restraining order. I had learned to set boundaries and limits on his behavior, meet with him in public places only, and not argue with him—and I wanted to give him a chance. Unbeknownst to me, he had a girlfriend with whom he was living, and with her interventions and care, he had settled down a bit. At times he still acts psychotic, but I always have an escape route—refusing to engage in his delusional thinking, and terminating conversations to protect myself from getting upset. As of this writing, living without a restraining or no-harassment order has worked out. My heart no longer aches to know how James is or whether he's safe. Most of the credit goes to his girlfriend. I've shared with her my strategies of setting boundaries and limits with him, and I've reiterated them several times to make sure she's safe. She has wisely installed a telephone landline, just in case she needs help in the event that her cell phone is dead.

Shortly after losing both my husband and my mother, another rather upsetting event occurred involving my older son, Edward, and *his* son, Nathan, who was eleven at the time. Since his mother and father, though separated, had joint custody, Nathan was accustomed to visiting his father every Tuesday evening, and the two of them would go to Nathan's karate lesson and then to a Chinese restaurant for dinner. Since Edward was working very hard as a painter and was in a relationship with a new girlfriend, Susan, it wasn't unusual for him to be exhausted at the end of the day. On the evening in question, Ed took Nate out for their evening meal and then fell asleep on the couch in the basement apartment that Arthur and I had built years earlier for Ed and his wife and baby Nathan. At 7:00 that evening, when I arrived home from work, Nate was trying to wake up his father, who was supposed to be returning Nathan to his mother at their rendezvous point, a nearby gas station. Ed was cursing at Nate because he wanted to sleep a little longer. Nate came up from the basement crying because of Ed's loud use of foul language. Trying to comfort him, I held him gently in my arms, telling him how much I loved him and that I would take him to the gas station so that he could be returned to his mother as planned. I was trying to help Ed, because Nate's mother could get out of control when she disapproved of Ed's behavior. After Nate calmed down, we got in my car and left for the gas station. En route, I got a call from Ed, who started screaming at me, telling me that I obviously didn't care about him or how he appeared in the eyes of others. He crowned this tirade with the observation that I apparently simply wanted to be an awesome grandmother and shouldn't have driven Nate to the gas station. Ed was screaming so loudly on the other end of the line that young Nate could hear what his father was saying. Trying to downplay the situation after I hung up, I told Nate that I was "in the dog house," which caused him to smile without further comment.

After delivering Nate to his mother at the gas station, I returned home to discover that Ed was gone. Although I was upset with him, I decided not to mention his abusive comments to me. I'd had a long day at work, and the continued strain of dealing with my sons' behavior, even though James was now out of the house, was taking its toll on me. Upset about everything that had occurred, and having no appetite for dinner, I decided to rest on the couch and invite no further contretemps. Forty-five minutes later, Edward returned home and proceeded to blast me again, repeating his verbal attack. Although I kept trying to tell him that I was simply trying to be helpful and had no intentions of making him look like a bad father, he angrily stated that I would no longer be allowed to see Nate on Tuesday nights or weekends, but that I *might* be able to see him on Mother's Day and Christmas. I was crushed, as I was extremely close to my grandson.

This put me into a tailspin. Having lost my husband and my mother to death and my younger son to schizophrenia, I was now being depriving of my *grandson*! My mood dropped through the floor. However, I had enough inner strength to tell Edward that, due to his attitude, he would have to be out of the house at the end of the month. It was not quite obvious to me at the time that I was pushing away another person in my life, but I knew I was not going to put up with verbal abuse and hurtful behavior any longer—from anyone. I'd been through enough pain in my life, and I couldn't tolerate any more.

Feeling both depressed and suicidal, and no longer able to tolerate or deal with the multiple losses, stresses, and arguments that overwhelmed me, I entered the hospital the next day for a two-week stay. Although I was in a great deal of psychological pain, the staff modified my medications and recommended that I have a meeting with Edward. Since I was extremely apprehensive about what Edward might say to me, the social worker suggested a supervised meeting with the nursing staff. That being agreed upon, the social worker called Edward and set up a meeting to be held a few nights later. Edward and his girlfriend, Susan, came, bringing some pastries from Mike's Bakery from the North End. The meeting offered me the opportunity to tell Ed that I was presently hospitalized because I loved Nate so much that being forbidden to be with him was psychologically intolerable. While Ed agreed to let me continue to see Nate, he seemed incapable of apologizing for the things he had said, and he actually denied that he had vowed to keep Nate away from me. Sometime later, during a conversation Ed and I were having, I reminded him of his inability to apologize to Nate and me. In response, he said, "Don't you remember when Susan and I visited you in the hospital and we brought you pastries?"

After I was discharged from the psychiatric hospital, my group therapist, Geri, helped me realize that Edward may never have been able to verbalize an apology, so he chose instead to visit me, with an offering of pastries as an olive branch.

With the passage of time, Edward and I are on better terms. Although it's like walking on eggshells, I try to be thoughtful and helpful while limiting the types of questions I ask him, for he doesn't hesitate to say what he thinks, no matter how abrasive he may seem. I'm careful how I phrase any questions. If Edward happens to be out of work for a period of time, I will ask if he needs anything like food or money, to which he'll reply, "Everything's fine." I don't often ask Ed to do work-related things for me, like hanging up curtain rods or putting up a shelf, but when I do, I generally pay him for his efforts. He's not at all affectionate toward me; he hugs me only when I ask for a hug on rare occasions like my birthday or Mother's Day. Unless he needs me to do something for him, such as babysitting, he never calls. When I moved to Framingham, about twelve minutes away from Ed's home in Natick, I asked him if I could attend Mass with him, since I'm his oldest daughter's godmother and I take that responsibility seriously. Never missing a beat, Ed instantly said no, with no further explanation. Though I felt his response was both unwarranted and hurtful, I suppose he saw my simple offer of help as interference in his life. Unlike other families, we are not really a close-knit group. I have friends who regularly go to church with their children, after which they go out to breakfast together—it's their family routine. They also do other things together on a daily basis and definitely talk with each other several times a day. I had hoped this would be my situation too, but it isn't.

Having recovered from Edward's emphatic no, I decided to continue going to services with my other godchild, whose home and church, St. John the Evangelist, are both in Cambridge. Not only do I take her with me, but I also enjoy singing in the church's choir. I feel appreciated there, and over time I've developed many close friendships. The organist is outstanding, and the choir director is amazing. The singing gives a lot of personal peace and inspiration, which is good therapy for both my spirit and my psyche.

In 2013, I moved from Cambridge to the town next to Edward's to be closer to him and his family. I wanted to be more available for transporting Nate (who now lives with Edward) to tae kwon do, and to be more available to Ed, his girlfriend, and their two children, my lovely and delightful granddaughters. I also made a fair amount of money on the sale of my Cambridge condominium. It may not be enough to live on for the rest of my life, but it has put extra money in the bank, earning an incredibly low rate of interest!

I haven't said many complimentary things about Edward, but he has always been there for me when I needed him. One evening after Arthur died, I told Ed that I was not feeling very well physically and wasn't able to do anything to help myself. I asked him to get me a cup of tea, which he did, and he also sat with me and watched Comedy Central on TV, which I genuinely appreciated. Also, just a few days prior to Arthur's death, I asked Ed if he would stay at his father's bedside while I took a break to go home, take a shower, and put on fresh clothes. There was no question of his willingness to relieve me. There have been other times too when he has been quite supportive. In September 2013, I had heart surgery for arrhythmia that couldn't be medically controlled, and then I was in rehab for three weeks due to an unexpected complication. Ed visited me almost every evening, either watching TV or playing cards with me, and he often brought me iced tea from Dunkin' Donuts, which I loved. I'm always thankful that I can depend upon him in delicate and critical situations.

An excellent painter, Ed once redid my condo in Cambridge as a Christmas-birthday present. It looked beautiful, and many people admired his meticulous work, which led to a few contract jobs for him as well. He also fixed the front bumper on my Honda Civic for another Christmas-birthday present.

Being a widow has always felt like a lonely journey. When Arthur was alive, we'd talk about everything, make decisions together, and be there for each other. Though it wasn't a perfect marriage, it was a good one, and I would marry him again if given the chance, for we loved each other. Although I have been emotionally ill for much of my life, I've always tried to push through life's obstacles, fulfilling the various roles I've been required to play. It wasn't easy, especially when it came to our children, since Arthur was the good cop and I was the bad cop. He would say that since I was the teacher, the nurse, and the mother, I could take care of the children, the house, the laundry, the lawn, and so forth, as well as work full-time.

Although I was faced with a multitude of responsibilities when my husband was alive, I still find it difficult being a widow and having to make decisions without him. But with the help of friends, doctors, therapists, and prayers for God's infinite guidance, I've managed to navigate the deepest of waters, even making financial decisions alone. Because Arthur had so many medical problems, he was never able to get life insurance. Consequently, I've had to work and figure out how to make ends meet, while my children are under the impression that I can still afford to do what we did as a couple, despite the fact that I'm a widow on disability and Medicare. Of course, the disability ceased when I turned sixty-five. I am able to collect some of my retirement from the wonderful hospital where I worked, although it is not a significant sum, since I worked there only thirteen years. Because I took time off for three maternity leaves and worked only part-time for a short period before I had to resign due to mental illness in 1989, I ended up just short of the ten full years of work required for me to be vested at community hospital in New Jersey.

One of the good things about being a widow is that no one is watching over my shoulder, telling me what I am allowed (or *not* allowed) to say. I resented this behavior on Arthur's part, and I would tell him that I needed to validate my thinking. If I had a problem, I wanted to share it with a friend and discuss various opinions and options. Arthur tried to control my voice our entire life together, especially after he was diagnosed with hemochromatosis. Being a very proud man, he didn't want anyone at work to know he was sick. Even after he started to become very confused, he insisted on going to work. While I respected his desire for privacy, he was an estimator who worked with large numbers, and I thought keeping his illness a secret was not in his or his company's best interest. One day when he was really confused driving to work, I called Paul, one of his best buddies, and asked him to call me at work any time if he noticed Arthur acting inappropriately or not thinking clearly. After that, I felt better, knowing that Paul would keep an eye on Arthur and wouldn't allow him to embarrass himself at work. As it turned out, Paul was one of the fellows who saw Arthur through his illness, calling him on the phone frequently and coming to my aid, along with another of Arthur's friends, within minutes of his death.

After Arthur died, I was hospitalized with mental illness four times. Very often I felt suicidal, frustrated, depressed, incompetent, upset, angry, hurt, hollow, sad, weary, exhausted, alone, unloved, fearful, anxious, and a whole lot of other adjectives relevant to a wounded mind. I had been diagnosed with major depressive disorder and received myriad medications, countless ECT treatments, and years of individual and group psychotherapy, and I attended two partial programs of about six weeks each. For about two years, I also attended meetings sponsored by the National Alliance for the Mentally Ill. Most of the people at those meetings suffered from depression, bipolar disorder, or personality disorder. There was also a group for families and patients with schizophrenia or related illnesses, but it turned out that those meetings were held quite a distance from my home, so I was unable to participate.

My job as a research nurse in the Brain Tumor Center was exhausting, and I felt unappreciated trying to do all that was expected of me while dealing with severe sadness and grief. With the added stress my sons were creating, I decided to change jobs in 2006, thinking that a different venue would be less stressful. The October after Arthur's death, I transferred to radiation oncology and worked there for almost two years, during which time I experienced myriad catastrophic events with James while dealing with my mother's problems as well. These events brought me to my knees and resulted in one of my hospitalizations after my mother died. Although I had received an Excellence in Nursing Award and been recertified as an oncology nurse, my head nurse lost faith in me after that hospitalization and my subsequent time off to attend a partial program. It's my belief that had I been absent from work for six or seven weeks with a physical illness, I would have been welcomed back with open arms—I would have received flowers, cards, and possibly even visits from the nursing staff. However, being absent with a *mental* illness was another story; even medical professionals lose trust and confidence in the mentally ill professional, regardless of how well he or she is when back on the job. There's a huge stigma associated with mental illness in our society. Most people don't know how to react to those afflicted with depression, grief, PTSD, agitated depression, or anxiety. You'd think that healthcare professionals would have a better understanding of people who have had to deal with depression and its symptoms. Unfortunately, this is far from the case; if anything, healthcare professionals are less empathetic than society in general.

Having been away from work for several weeks, and still dealing with anxiety and depression, I asked to return to work part-time for about three weeks. However, my head nurse told me, "Brain tumor patients need to have a nurse who is reliable, not someone who is here part-time," and she placed a nurse who had been dealing with lung cancer patients in my position. This move seemed irrational to me. I had been working with brain tumor patients for nine years; all I needed was a chance to prove myself. Being replaced had a profound effect on my self-confidence, resulting in further emotional upset and depression.

I suspect that one of my coworkers may have influenced the head nurse's decision to demote me to the position of a fill-in nurse on the unit. There was a radiation oncologist, a specialist in neuro-oncology, who would refer to people with any sort of mental issue as "crazy" and would have nothing to do with them. He would have the nurse and the fellow see such patients and report their findings to him prior to his very hasty visit with the patient. I'm convinced of such subterfuge because around that same time, one of the *other* neuro-radiation oncologists considered my work outstanding and nominated me as "best in the department"—an award I didn't receive, but a nomination that meant a lot to me because someone had seen that I had worked hard to cover up my many bouts of depression and had tried to be the best nurse possible. The difference in the two doctors' perspectives was amazing.

Although I eventually went back full-time after a few weeks of part-time work, having been relegated to a fill-in position was a disappointment. Feeling somewhat disrespected and isolated by my peers, I chose to leave the Department of Radiation Oncology and return to the Brain Tumor Center.

I was warmly welcomed back there as a "generalist," which was fine with me, as I didn't want to be responsible for research patients and all the work associated with them. The position involved preparing summaries of new patients for the neuro-oncologists. We dealt with a variety of disorders, including neurofibromatosis, Waldenstrom macroglobulinemia syndrome, brain lymphoma, and benign and malignant tumors, especially glioblastomas. Unfortunately, completing insurance forms for these patients was stressful, because insurance companies would not pay until the summaries were completed, despite the patients' need for money. (I felt bad about this, because I knew how important the money was to families dealing with a brain tumors.)

There were times when dealing with insurance companies was fatiguing, for they were often reluctant to pay for certain chemotherapy drugs that were very expensive but only somewhat effective. One day I had to spend eight hours on the phone with an insurance company to obtain authorization of payment for a single drug that cost $25,000 a dose. The patient's family would call me intermittently to check on my headway, understandably upset that I could not obtain authorization more quickly. However, I ultimately got permission for the patient to receive the medication.

I also regularly drew blood on patients because I was a "good stick" most of the time, and I helped out with research patients who needed injections or their drug reactions measured. I did the tasks other people didn't have time to do, while also attending to my own medical and psychological needs. My frequent doctor and therapist appointments meant I spent considerable extra hours working during the week and on weekends to accomplish my hospital assignments, rather than using my earned time for personal appointments. I was very grateful to the hospital for allowing me flexibility on these occasions. The nurse practitioners showed sincere concern for me; they were aware of my bouts with deep-seated depression and my problems on the home front, to which the requirements of my job added even more stress.

My mood would vary on its own accord, with or without provocation—or so it seemed. I felt like I was on an eternal seesaw, for my mood would plummet every two weeks or so. Even when I was feeling better, I was apprehensive, always waiting for the other shoe to drop. I knew my son James was a big part of the problem, but there was more to it than that. It was as if something inside me were pulling me down. I got to the point where I not only couldn't sleep, but also had no energy, despite taking the stimulant Provigil (often used for narcolepsy). Even with the augmentations made by my psychiatrist, Dr. Dave, my medications were not working well. I was finding it difficult to deal with anything, including the ride to work, which I thought I had fixed by selling my house and buying a two-bedroom condominium in Cambridge. Dr. Dave had told me that I needed to be closer to the hospital, because the two-hour commute each way was far too long on top of my long, stressful workdays. So I moved to Cambridge in September 2009, but by January 2010, I'd completely lost it; I begged Dr. Dave to admit me to the hospital, because I could no longer cope with anything. I even forgot how to do my needlepoint, which I'd always used for therapeutic relaxation. (I had been working on a particular piece for months, a Christmas stocking for my granddaughter who was to be born in April.) I constantly felt suicidal, but despite the variety of ways in which I planned to accomplish this release, I never attempted any of them. Yet I seriously wanted to die in order to escape the emotional and painful life I was living. In my desperation, I was unable to function in *any* area, and so my doctor arranged for me to be admitted to a major teaching hospital, and eventually I was started on ECT again, continuing treatments for six months. I received very little benefit from them, even though this time I was given medicine to help me avoid the memory loss I experienced from my first round of ECT in 1990.

Arthur chauffeured me to and from that first round of treatments; now I was dependent upon other forms of transportation and other people. This was new for me, for I usually was independent (and helping others), and I'd depended upon my husband when he was well and I was in need. Edward and his girlfriend, Susan, helped me for months, picking me up after each ECT treatment. My daughter, Song, would visit me, and on occasion I would take a bus down to Brooklyn to visit her. By now I was psychologically unglued and able to accomplish very little. I had to stop driving, as I couldn't sort out what was going on with respect to traffic, especially when it came to traffic circles (or rotaries, as they refer to them in Massachusetts). I became dependent on the Ride, part of the Boston area's mass transit system, and I was grateful for the fact that it was both inexpensive and dependable. It took me to appointments and brought me home, picking up and dropping off two or three other clients along the way, which added time to the trips.

I spent a lot of time alone, and after my therapy group recommended that I get a dog or a cat, Song came up from Brooklyn and arranged for me to obtain a Himalayan Persian kitten I named Cambridge. On the way home from picking him up, I stopped to show him off at the home of a friend who loved animals, and she recognized that my kitten was very sick. So I immediately took him to Angel Veterinary Hospital, a facility associated with the veterinary school at Tufts University. The vet bill and the cost of the kitten exceeded my expectations, but I thought, *Oh well—it's only money,* a phrase my husband's cousin Ray was fond of saying. Cambridge was worth the cost, for he has brought me a lot of comfort over the last six years. I believe he thinks he is part dog, because he always greets me at the door when I come home.

Eventually I regained my emotional equilibrium to a point, but I continued to seesaw from time to time. I joined a widows' group whose members have all been through the same loss and grieving process, and I am very grateful for the many friendships I've made there. Here are some of the pearls of wisdom I've learned from them over the years: life changes radically once you become a widow; relationships change, and other couples who were your friends in the past drop out of the picture unless you reach out to them and they, in turn, are comfortable with you being single; and when you're associating with a couple, friction may occur if the wife becomes jealous of any attention her husband gives you. I've been blessed by the way my closest friends have stood by me. Fortunately, my closest friends and family members who would have helped me out if I'd asked them lived far away, so I did not experience any jealous conflicts.

For a widow, attending social functions may feel strange. For example, going to a wedding alone is often uncomfortable unless you are seated with the family. If you are going to invite a widow to a wedding or any similar function, it might be good to allow her to bring a guest. At two recent weddings, I brought my daughter and my cousin (who recently lost his wife); both times this worked out well for me. Many of the widows in my group say they go to wedding ceremonies but not to receptions because of the pain they generate. Also, if you're a widow, inviting couples to a dinner party can lead to days of crying after the party is over. I've had company over for dinner, but this usually includes a mix of family members, widows, and single friends. It's my recommendation to be mindful of the position you put yourself in before attending an event that might generate disappointment and sadness.

Widows and widowers are often told not to make any major changes during the first year after the death of a spouse. You will still celebrate birthdays, holidays, and anniversaries, but in a different fashion, and getting use to these changes takes time. The hard fact is your spouse will always be gone and won't return after the first year. You must navigate that year differently, sometimes accompanied by tears of sadness, feelings of loss, and memories of incidents now past. In many cases, adult children can be very attentive to you, but the opposite can be true too. It's important to take your time adjusting to the many changes that come with being a widow, and to heal at your own pace. Some people heal within months, while others never recover from the loss of a spouse. Everyone grieves differently too: some find solace in staying busy, while others must take some time before integrating into social situations.

I've found volunteering to be therapeutic in many ways, for it provides some structure to your life, and in giving you receive so much more in return. It also prevents isolation, which is an easy pattern to fall into when you're depressed and grieving for the lost company of a loved one. Volunteering as an ESL teacher has been rewarding for me, for it has opened my eyes to the rest of the world. There are many volunteer opportunities with nonprofit organizations. One of my widow friends who volunteers in a senior center has found that helping other seniors in need of company and day care is extremely rewarding.

Most of all, you need to take care of yourself. You may not have had the opportunity to do so in the past, but now it's quite possible that you have the time, especially if you don't have the responsibility of caring for young children. You may need some help getting started, especially if you have been a caretaker for most of your life. I was once in that category, and I was not aware of the importance of self-care and self-love. It took years of therapy for me to understand and implement these concepts. My family still sees me as a caretaker, but I now take the time I need for myself and the activities I want to engage in, such as choir, yoga, tai chi, exercise, writing, and group therapy. It's good to engage in activities that give you pleasure, for they encourage socialization. The practice of taking care of yourself doesn't mean you're totally self-absorbed and can't do for others; it means you've learned the importance of maintaining balance in life.

When I got married, I didn't expect my husband to die at an early age, even though my father died at the age of fifty-four. Early in our marriage, Arthur presented me with a Norman Rockwell sculpture of a little old couple in old-fashioned clothing sitting at a small, round table by a fireplace. There's a glint of love in their eyes as they enjoy a cup of tea. During our twenty-eight-year marriage, I adopted this figurine as the image of a dream I had for our relationship. I had expected that we'd retire together, grow old together, and enjoy our golden years together. But this was obviously not what God had in mind for us. Some widows react by getting angry at God when their dreams are altered and they are left behind. I never got angry at God or at my husband for leaving me a widow at the age of fifty-five. I knew that God had a plan for the balance of my life, and it didn't include my husband.

Arthur didn't ask to be born with a genetic disorder that would take his life at an early age. What upset me was that this genetic disorder was a part of his family's heredity, yet those afflicted with it never mentioned it to the rest of the family. Unlike my husband's cousins, who kept their disease a secret, Arthur told all his other cousins and urged them and their biological offspring to be tested for hemochromatosis. We had our own two boys tested, and we discovered that one is a carrier of the gene, but not afflicted, and the other isn't a carrier. The carrier, of course, needs to be mindful of the threat of hemochromatosis should he ever marry and have children—especially if his wife carries the same gene. Though it is a very debilitating and potentially deadly disease (like so many other genetic disorders), it's important for family members to know about it, because it can be managed when caught at an early age and stage.

In the case of finances, it's never too early to get whole life insurance. Since Arthur had hypertension and was really obese by his twenties, he didn't qualify for life insurance. And although we both had jobs, Arthur and I spent all our money on our homes and children, leaving nothing for retirement. Therefore when he died, I was left with considerable debt. Arthur had always taken care of the books, wanting to do so, no doubt, because he had been a banking and finance major in college. Fortunately I was able to take out a limited insurance policy on him through the hospital where I worked, and he had a similar one through his work, and so I had enough money to pay for the funeral, pay off our bills, underwrite Song's modest wedding, and help with moving expenses.

I had anticipated working until I was seventy, but God had different plans for me. In 2010, crippled by my illness, I left my job on disability at the age of fifty-nine. Even as I write this at the age of sixty-five, I find myself unable to work; I'm still drained of energy because of chronic fatigue syndrome. Anything that I might earn from a job would be deducted from my disability benefit, and so financially, physically, and psychologically, it's simply not in my best interest to return to work. I doubt I could work an eight-hour shift without succumbing to stress and exhaustion.

Unfortunately, while dealing with the mental issues, I've developed a few more medical problems, including fibromyalgia (which was nicely taken care of by acupuncture), spinal stenosis (which also responds to acupuncture), atrial fibrillation (for which I had heart surgery followed by serious postoperative complications), a torn rotator cuff (which is now fully healed following surgery), hyperparathyroidism (which also required surgery), a left knee replacement due to arthritis, Raynaud's disease, and hypothyroidism. I was supposed to have back surgery three years ago, but it was cancelled due to the rotator cuff surgery. (I would like to avoid back surgery if at all possible, because I am tired of having surgery.) However, I have already lost two inches in height from the spinal stenosis, and I might keep on shrinking, as my mother did. (She lost about five inches in height from her back issues.)

The hospital where I worked is very generous and allows disabled employees to continue to subscribe to its health plan and receive two-thirds of their salary until age sixty-five. (I purchased a disability policy through the hospital.) Now that I've aged out, I'm left with social security, my widow's benefit, and a pension commensurate with the thirteen years I worked at the hospital. I hope I'll have the energy in the future to do some part-time work—I have some ideas in mind—but right now I'm relying on God to watch over me and guide me day by day.

When you lose a spouse, grief is a real part of the healing process, especially if the relationship was a happy one. Some religious and hospice organizations have grief therapy groups, which can be helpful when you're ready to do your grief work. It might take a while to figure out when this should begin. I started six weeks after my husband died; others wait a whole year. If your grief turns into depression (and it sometimes does), you may need to seek help from a professional who specializes in grief counseling, such as a psychologist, licensed clinical social worker, rabbi, minister, priest, counselor, or psychiatrist. Some insurance plans will pay for a portion of this therapy; others may not. Either way, when you're struggling with profound sadness related to grief, it's worth the time and money to get the help you need and deserve. As my widow friend Kay said, "I can't think of anyone better to spend the money on than myself." This is a good philosophy to consider, since you are the most important person to take care of after your spouse dies—and if you don't take care of yourself, you can't be useful to anyone else.

The importance of taking care of me has been a lesson that's taken me years to learn, and now my own care is a full-time job! Yes, I volunteer and help my children and grandchildren, but I also enjoy the friends I have made via the widow's groups and the church choir. In 2013, I treated myself to a yoga retreat vacation in Mexico—the first time I'd gone on vacation by myself. I didn't know anyone at the start, but by the end of the trip I'd made a lot of new acquaintances. It was a wonderful experience, and I have no regrets about using my money to take care of *me*. I have no idea how much longer I will be able to do that sort of thing, so I'm doing things I can enjoy and benefit from *now*. It's like shopping at Marshalls: if you see it and like it, you'd better buy it *now*, for tomorrow it might not be there.

A college friend always ended our conversations with one word: "Enjoy!" So my advice to women (and men) in the midst of their new journey of widowhood is "Grieve as you must, but enjoy!"

Chapter 12

Dismemberment and a Miracle

$\mathcal{B}$etween November 2012 and January 2013, at the age of sixty-two, I felt totally hollow, like an empty shell. I was walking around aimlessly, without any purpose in life. I wasn't suicidal; I just couldn't tolerate the feelings of emptiness I was experiencing. It seemed my family had no use for me—or so I felt. I didn't understand why I was falling apart when I had made such incredible progress.

I told Dr. Dave that I felt like I was wandering around in the wilderness, like Moses did in the Old Testament, and that I was questioning the meaning of my life. I *begged* him to give me ECT. (I must have been out of my mind to make such a request, for I had had so many side effects from ECT in the past.) He gently explained that the ECT wouldn't help because I had a "hole" in my heart. Then he asked me if I would speak with a shaman.

Dr. Dave was working with another set of tools, of which I was unaware. I had encountered the word *shaman* in the book *Eat, Pray, Love* by Elizabeth Gilbert; her reference was to a medicine man in a remote village in the jungle. But Dr. Dave explained to me that he had a contact named Candice who lived in Connecticut. He gave me her full name and phone number, explaining that I could work with her over the telephone, and that I would need to confer with her only a few times. He also assured me that most shamans are modest, and that she wouldn't charge much. I had mixed feelings about contacting her, since I had no idea what I was getting myself into. So I went online to find out about shamans and what they did. Unfortunately, the online information was extremely sketchy, and I wasn't sure about the authenticity of their qualifications.

While I had tried almost everything my treating physicians suggested over the years, Dr. Dave was my first doctor to mix western and eastern medicine. Under his care, I tried yoga, meditation, relaxation, acupuncture, massage therapy, cognitive behavioral therapy (which is actually western in origin), and osteopathic manipulation. Yoga and meditation (prayer) produced significant positive effects on my mood and anxiety. With the introduction of eastern practices to traditional western medicine, I steadily improved. Yet despite all the progress I made via all these modalities, I still felt disheartened. Although I was skeptical and even fearful of working with a shaman—I didn't want to get involved with witch doctors or voodoo, because that was contrary to my religious faith—I thought, *What do I have to lose?* I decided to give it a try.

At first I had difficulty reaching Candice; Dr. Dave had given me the wrong phone number. Finally I e-mailed him and he gave me the correct number, and I eventually made contact with Candice in mid-January 2013. I briefly reviewed some of my mental history, after which we spoke for about forty-five minutes. Then Candice went to work.

My doctor diagnosed me as having a broken heart. (I'm sure this diagnosis isn't in the DSM IV or V). In shamanic terms, this state of being is considered a form of dismemberment. In their 2010 book, *Awakening into the Spirit World*, Sandra Ingerman and Hank Wesselman describe the process of dismemberment as being stripped of all skin, muscles, and organs until nothing is left but the skeleton. Although this process sounds violent, there's no pain involved. This is the initiation to the shamanic path, and it provides a formidable form of healing, because at the end of the dismemberment experience, you are reassembled by a helping spirit, but with all the distortions and illnesses left out. It's a classic way to achieve a new, luminous energy body that is free of the burdens you've been carrying around for much of your life. In a dismemberment experience, you may also lose your ego and your sense of separateness from the power of the universe. It's a death experience, yet it's also an experience of reconnection, of recalling your true origins as a pure spirit. The dismemberment experience is often a wonderful gift, a kind of liberation, the authors say. The egoic, self-possessed individual must die so that a new self may be born (216-218).

According to Ingerman and Wesselman, "the dismemberment experience is a level of initiation followed by a feeling and vision of the body being renewed and by the acquisition of magical or healing powers." This usually happens to those who become shamans, they note, adding, "The transformation of the physical being into light is seen everywhere as a spiritual rebirth in which the visionary becomes a luminous being who has access to the spirits and spiritual realm."

Wesselman writes,

> The light that is in us is the light and love of the universe. To make the direct transformative connection with our immortal spiritual aspect through the path of direct revelation is to experience a sense of extraordinary perfection accompanied by an overwhelming feeling of love. When Jesus of Nazareth proclaimed, "I am the light," the message was actually "You and I and all of us are the light." Our immortal soul aspect is the light and love beyond form.

On January 10, 2013, I wrote in my journal that I was very unhappy and that I had been praying to God for some insight regarding the meaning of my existence. Dr. Dave would have said that the universe came together—that is, God was the cause of my feelings of emptiness. Religiously speaking, Christ states that we must die to be reborn. I wasn't sure what was going on inside me; I simply knew that I was empty, living a life without meaning and filled with despair—a state of being that, oddly enough, followed several months of intensive therapy with very good results. No doubt some of the feelings I was experiencing were generated by my sense that my children didn't need me, especially during the holiday season. Though I'd made great progress dealing with many of the problems in my life, the feelings I'd begun to experience this time were greater and different than any I'd experienced during all those years of mental illness.

On January 15, 2013, I had my first conversation with Candice over the telephone. Dr. Dave had notified her that I would be calling, and he'd given her a very limited amount of information about me. He simply told her that I was resistant to all treatments. During our conversation, Candice used a crystal pendulum and charts to gather information. She was in a spiritual trance, yet totally present to our conversation. I later wrote in my journal that I thought she must have been receiving spiritual messages. At the beginning of our conversation, she asked me a few questions about my physical health— questions that were so reflective of my recent medical experiences that I was in awe of her insight. She asked me about my neck; I'd had parathyroid surgery the previous September. Then she asked about my lower back, which had caused me significant discomfort because of spinal stenosis. In the course of our conference, I mentioned that I hated confrontation, to which she replied, "From this point on, you can speak what's on your heart, because it's important to *both* people in the conversation to know what the other is thinking." When she said this, I felt liberated. At last I had found my voice; I had the power to verbalize my thoughts and was no longer afraid to share them. Her comments led to a change in my behavior—not that I went around ranting, but I simply spoke my mind, in a kind way. In essence, we were off to an amazing start.

Candice said that spirits from a past life and the earlier years of my present life were preventing me from going forward. I wasn't quite sure about her reference to reincarnation, but I could accept the notion of spirits invading my being during *this* lifetime. She also said that spirits or discarnates (spirits or energy forces without bodies) from other people's lives had entered my vulnerable body over the years. At that point, I thought things were getting weird. She indicated that there was a lot of darkness around me and there were many discarnates within my being. She noted the appearance of a very large "poser"—a dark person or ghost or spirit—standing behind me. I suggested that it was my father, but Candice said it wasn't him. Then I mentioned Chris, my friend who had committed suicide. She didn't think it was Chris either; she said she would have to study this more. She added that the discarnates needed to be cut and burned—that the contracts I had made with these spirits had to be terminated forever, and that I needed to be guaranteed that none of them would enter my body again. Candice said that if she could not clear all the spirits, she would send me to someone who worked with Saint Michael the Archangel. I was wondering if she was talking about exorcism—for which I was definitely not ready—because I had read something about exorcism when I did my initial research on shamanism.

Though I am Roman Catholic, I wasn't sure of the role of Saint Michael the Archangel, so I once again went online, and to my amazement I found the following prayer:

> St. Michael the Archangel, defend us in battle.
> Be our protection against the wickedness and the snares
> of the Devil.
> May God rebuke him, we humbly pray;
> And do Thou, O Prince of the Heavenly Host—

By the Divine Power of God
Cast into Hell, Satan and all evil spirits
Who roam throughout the world, seeking the ruin of
souls.
Amen.

I knew there were several mentions of Saint Michael the Archangel in the Old and New Testaments—specifically in the books of Daniel, Jude, and Revelation. I have also been to a friend's Catholic church where they say the above prayer after every morning Mass. I found it scary to think there were spirits roaming the earth, trying to invade our souls and our bodies.

Candice, my shaman, said that in my earlier life there had been a lot of trauma and self-punishment, and that I needed to love myself. She suggested that I imagine a cool, white light entering the top of my head; a blue light entering my kidneys, the center of strength; and a pink light entering my heart, the center of love and kindness. She added that the pink light could be as expansive as I wanted it to be. She instructed me to pray when I woke up in the middle of the night, since this was a time to get some work done, and she suggested that I eat pears to relieve the grief that was stored in my lungs. That night I did my shamanic exercises (or rituals), and what came through was a very clear message that I should love myself, which was revelatory, confirming, and thrilling. I began doing these rituals on a regular basis, and soon they felt meditative in nature. That evening during our phone call, Candice told me that a spirit entered my body when I was five years old, thwarting my ability to be playful. I believe she was absolutely right. I never told her anything about my early childhood—she was simply clairvoyant. She encouraged me to think of everything as play, even though I was an adult. She also told me that when I was an infant, the spirit of arthritis entered my being. As I previously stated, I started having symptoms of osteoarthritis at the age of seventeen.

I followed all Candice's instructions, just as I'd always followed the instructions of my doctors and therapists throughout the years, with the exception my initial rejection of ECT. Within a few days I felt like a totally new person—happy, peaceful, smiling, lighthearted, and no longer concerned with the purpose of my life. I felt completely free of the burdens that had depressed me from November to mid-January. I believe it was a miracle that I no longer felt lost in a wilderness of darkness, but rather was reborn in the light. It was truly hard to believe how much my perceptions of the world and the spirit within me had changed. I firmly believe that God used Candice and Dr. Dave as my healers and His helpers. Indeed, if Jesus allowed His disciples and the apostles to perform healing miracles, why couldn't He use Candice and Dr. Dave the same way? I thanked Candice, Dr. Dave, and God *profusely* for the miracle that had been performed in my life. Every night I thank God for this miracle and incredible blessing, and I pray for the well-being of all those who are treating me.

On January 18, the day after I spoke with Candice the second time, I had an appointment with Dr. Dave. He immediately perceived and was thrilled with the change in my mood, personality, countenance, and thinking. He told me that there was a good possibility that I'd never have depression again. I could hardly believe that such a miracle was possible. However, concerned with the manner in which I'd been healed, I spoke with a nun who is a spiritual director. Sister Catherine advised me that God can use all kinds of people as His vessels in the healing of His children. After her reassurance, I felt more at ease.

On January 21, 2013, I again spoke with Candice, who had done a lot of work in the meantime, having cleared thousands of discarnates. She said that after the first spirit came out, thousands of other spirits followed. Furthermore, she informed me that I'd lost two pieces of my soul: the first loss was to arthritis when I was five months old, and the second loss occurred when I was five years old and lost the ability to play. Advising me to think of *everything* as play, Candice told me about "soul retrieval"—the way to retrieve those lost parts of my soul. She recommended that I communicate with these restored parts, becoming familiar with them and learning how to take care of them. Having done so, I can tell you that, as of this writing, my spinal stenosis has gotten better with acupuncture and the arthritis in my knees has diminished somewhat as well. Also, I am learning to play with my grandchildren and enjoy everything I do, even if it's cleaning the bathrooms, because the end result is that the child inside of me is happy—or the bathroom looks better. That's pleasure!

Candice told me that she was going to do some long-distance acupuncture to clear my liver, noting that it was congested because of all the drugs I'd been taking. She advised me to drink warm lemon water and olive oil, but quite frankly I forgot about that. She also suggested that I try soaking my feet in Epsom salts for relaxation, and that I start exercising, which I now do in the form of yoga, cycling, and water aerobics.

Both Dr. Dave and Candice weighed in on the role of Chris, my dear friend who committed suicide. While they agreed that Chris had a role in my life, they were of differing opinions about that role. Candice thought that Chris was brought into this world to lead the way for me and help me along life's journey. Dr. Dave thought Chris and I were twins in the sense that we had had deeply similar relationships and thoughts. Despite having felt suicidal many times in my life, I never acted upon that impulse, and I have often felt that Chris, like a guardian angel, helped me through those periods of severe depression and grief.

Dr. Dave believed that I had gone through the process of dismemberment, which he thought was wonderful. I really *had* felt like an empty shell wandering around in the wilderness. While this was psychologically upsetting and painful, it was not physically painful. The reassembly was done through the spiritual work of Candice.

As I write this, three years have passed, and my mood has never dropped for more than a day or two. True, I have been sad at times, which is normal and healthy. On occasion, when thinking about the loss of my husband or mother—especially when I am sharing something about one of them with another person—I may get weepy, but my mood remains solid.

In September 2013, I had cardiac surgery, and afterward I was very ill with unremitting postoperative atrial fibrillation. Although I received excellent nursing care, no one seemed concerned that I didn't eat or drink much for more than a week. I was convinced that I was going to die, and while I wasn't afraid, I actually wanted to *live* for a change. So despite the fact that I was weak from the surgery, this realization caused a turnabout in my recovery. My good mood maintained itself, which had never been the case previously.

I also worked with another shaman near where I live in Massachusetts, Dr. John, who attempted to get to the root of some issues I had never totally dealt with, such as forgiving my father and maintaining a loving heart for my son James. One day shortly after our work began, I experienced a rather dark energy that scared me—it felt smothering, sinister, and overwhelming. However, I worked through it by constantly praying to Mary, Mother of God, to help me love myself so that I could love James. I am not certain why I chose this route, but Mary is an example of a loving mother, and so I thought her love would conquer the darkness I felt. Some say that while darkness is the opposite of light, it is not a bad thing in and of itself. Nevertheless, this dark energy (not depression) felt like a negative experience to me.

I worked with Dr. John for a few months, but I never felt connected to him. As usual, I tried to follow his directions and do what he asked of me, but I felt no benefit from working with him, and so I stopped.

Dr. Dave sent me to another shaman in a more distant town to see if I was destined to become a shaman and to inquire about some herbal supplements. I chose not to talk with this shaman about herbal supplements; I was taking enough medicine already and did not want to add to the mix. But I did speak with him about becoming a shaman, although I did not see this in my future. He said that I would become a helper, not a shaman, and that I would be in demand. He also spoke of the importance of water, saying that I should collect vials of water from different locations. I smiled when he said that, because I have some holy water and my husband loved being around the water. With respect to my being a helper, it was unclear to me how this role would manifest itself; I'd always been a caretaker. Recently, I have been a helper with family needs, but I am always mindful of Dr. Dave's admonishment not to help others at my own expense.

Dr. Dave is presently in the process of slowly tapering off my medications. Being a very wise physician, he is instantly responsive if I report any change that wasn't present prior to lowering a dose. For example, after he slowly lowered my dose of Abilify, my chronic fatigue became more pronounced,but my mood remained stable. I had to return to a slightly higher dose in order to reduce my fatigue. I'm so thankful that I have a bright, sensitive, knowledgeable psychiatrist who is also a shaman.

I pray every day to thank God for the miracle He performed for me, leading me into the light through both the Holy Spirit and the wonderful people He's placed in my life. Without such a team, I'd probably be dead. But I now want to live, taking one day at a time and taking care of myself while doing whatever God wants me to do.

I've recounted these experiences to inspire others with mental or physical illnesses to find people who can help them, and to let them know that there is a healing world that exists outside traditional medicine. I hope this account will bring hope and faith to those who suffer and will help them realize that each one of us has a purpose in this world. I have learned and sincerely believe that all things work together for the good of those who love the Lord, and that there are no coincidences in life.

It's also my hope and desire that the traditional medical community will come to recognize these alternative ways of healing and will incorporate them into their alternative medicine curriculum. Research has already shown the benefits of acupuncture and yoga, and I recently heard the story of a mother who went from shaman to shaman until her son was cured of his schizophrenia. Some of these practices have been around for centuries, and they have survived because many of them work. I'm an example of the benefits of a combination of western and eastern medicine, shamanism and faith in God; all of them have led to the healing of the hole in my heart.

For years I had lived in darkness due to soul loss and the invasion of my being by discarnates. Now I'm living in the light, which allows me to deal with my issues in healthier ways. It does not dismiss the trauma, grief, and anxiety I've experienced throughout my life, but now I look at these events and realize I'm healthier and stronger because I've experienced them. Each day brings new challenges and problems, of course, and sometimes there's a resurgence of old feelings of sadness, pain, and trauma. But I've found that prayer, meditation, shamanic journeying, and asking for the wisdom to solve my issues help me gain insight into them and resolve my intense feelings. I've also learned that it's important to ask others for their prayers, especially when my spirit is troubled. In turn, it's important to pray for others when *they* have issues. Meditation also leads to connection with the Holy Spirit, who in many cases can be instrumental in the resolution of issues. Perhaps someday I can help others in the way *I've* been helped—sharing the faith, hope and love *I've* experienced—and thereby be a source of light to them. May anyone reading this account also find the joy *I've* experienced by living in the light.

Epilogue

*I*t is now July 2016. In January 2016, I celebrated my third anniversary without agitated depression, anxiety, PTSD, or complicated grief. I still miss my husband and my mother, who as of March 2016 have been dead ten years and eight years, respectively. James no longer haunts me, as I began blocking his calls after he gave me a very difficult time when I attempted to turn over to him the title of the car that I completely paid for during the summer of 2015. Sometimes I hear from his former girlfriend, but their relationship is very complicated. Unfortunately, she left him because he became verbally abusive and physically threatening. I don't blame her one bit.

Edward has a successful painting business; however, he calls me only to ask me to babysit. This still distresses me, because I need to know that he loves me as a person and not just a reliable babysitter. Song is now the mother of an eighteen-month-old girl who is both beautiful and delightful.

In June 2015, I started work on my master's in counseling. I am doing very well with online courses from Grand Canyon University in Phoenix, Arizona; overall, they seem to be a natural fit for me. I look forward to completing the intensive program in about two and a half years so I can help others as I have been helped, but on a limited basis. Presently I am on hiatus; the academic work became too intense, and as life would have it, I was needed to help my family with many different issues, especially the care of my grandson, Nathan. I plan to go back to school after this book is published.

As for my medical health, I had my left knee replaced in March 2015 and have resumed yoga and cycling. I am slower than I used to be, but I am progressing. Unfortunately, I remain saddled with chronic fatigue syndrome, but this is something I have to live with. Every day I need to rest from two to five times, but I never get restorative sleep except at night, and only after taking a complicated regimen of medications. The spinal stenosis acts up when I overdo it; acupuncture helps, but it is not covered by health insurance. I continue attending weekly group therapy, and I see Geri on a monthly basis for individual work. Dr. Holly has retired. I miss her as a person and an excellent therapist. I continue to see Dr. Dave once a month. We are still trying to get me off of some of my medications, which is no easy feat; however, we are making slow and steady progress. He also helps me resolve big issues as they come along. My faith in God continues, and I remain grateful for my healing. I have been blessed with many friends in my church choir and my widows' group.

I have started working on another book while I wait for this one to be edited and published. This is in addition to the many hours I spend with my schoolwork and helping others. Additionally, I make sure I have some fun every day by participating in activities and exercises.

Candice and I see each other from time to time when I pass through Connecticut. She remains an amazing person. I periodically participate in shamanic journeying, and I always find very helpful answers to life's problems.

I am very grateful to all the people who have helped and encouraged me to write this book. I hope that they will find benefits and hope in reading about finding the light.

The following and final comment was one I heard from Deacon Roland Rugoletti, who was the husband of a dear friend of mine. (An interesting note: he died within a couple of days of my husband.) He was very active as a scoutmaster, and he often made this remark to his Boy Scouts:

"Hope I have brought a little light into your life."

Peace to all.

Printed in the United States
By Bookmasters